DISTANT STORY BLUE

A family, a boat, an adventure at sea

MAGDALENA LOUISE HIRT

Sea Crow Press

Distant Story Blue: A family, a boat, an adventure at sea

Published 2024 by Sea Crow Press
Barnstable, MA
www.seacrowpress.com

First Edition

Paperback ISBN: 978-1-961864-16-0
Ebook ISBN: 978-1-961864-17-7
Library of Congress Control Number: 2024909820

Cover Image: Magdalena Louise Hirt
Sea view engraving ID 128130432,
Background © Yurii Romanovich | Dreamstime.com
Interior and Cover Design: Mary Petiet

Contents

When the knot is tied right
it hangs perfectly on the lifeline. Just like
the plan that stretches on a string across a map
that becomes a boat drifting over the waves—

Sail away.

for the ocean and her sprouted islands

Pre-Dawn Secrets

INTRODUCTION TO OUR SAILING LIFE

Pull anchor up from a tiny stone bay with a cave. Sail softly over the sea so calm and eerie, silver and slithering still. Drop anchor cozy and snug at an empty island you've been reading about surrounded with cliffs and birds. Walk the huge rocks off the shore that contain so many stories of survival, exploration, and history. Feel magic in the moment. Pull anchor again and head north with hot tea in hand finding room on the sea.

To sail is to feel these directions in as many moments in as many days as possible. We go from place to place begging our soul to digest enough, asking our mind to absorb enough, wanting time to explore enough. We will always ask, "Is it time to move on? Have I held this moment in my mind so that when I sail away, I can still smell it or taste it?" But we move, and most of the magic is in the moving.

I was raised in the dunes that follow the shore of Lake Michigan. I would set up camp in the woods and look off into the distance as far as I could see. I knew there was land across the endlessness that was unreachable with my land legs. This began my love of sailboats, and the magic a hull and sail offered to sweep me to otherwise unattainable locations.

After my undergraduate degree in poetry, a thirst for travel possessed me, and I bought a van, tore out the seats for a bed, and traveled the States for the next two years. Shortly thereafter, I earned my teaching degree, and married a sailor. Living a life with a house and schedule ended when I was homeschooling four children and my husband, Nick, became mobile in his work.

On Father's Day of 2017, our family of six moved to a boat in the Caribbean that had only been seen by my husband. My youngest was in diapers and still breastfeeding. *Selkie*, our 49 ft Westerly, tied at a marina, awaited the adventure that has continued for six years. We have sailed up and down the Caribbean Islands, across the North Atlantic via Bermuda and the Azores, explored Ireland, wintered in Scotland, ping ponged between the Outer Hebrides and Skye up to Shetland and over to Norway, traversed the Skagerrak and Kattegat to Denmark, circled the Baltic Sea and visited Russia, crossed the English Channel to Southern England where we quarantined during Covid, crossed the Bay of Biscay, visited multiple locations in Glacia, Spain, sailed to the Canary Islands, Cape Verde, back to the Caribbean, stopped in the Dominican Republic, stayed in Guatemala for hurricane season, explored the Yucatán, enjoyed Panama and the canal to reach the Pacific, swam with sharks and sea lions in the Galapagos, spent twenty-three days at sea to reach the Marquesas, slipped into the atolls of the Tuamotus, enjoyed the dancers in Tahiti and the drums of Moorea, stayed protected from storms in Bora Bora, dove deep into the caves of Tonga, spent a Christmas at sea on the way to New Zealand, battled the winds and waves of the southern hemisphere for seven months in New Zealand's North and South Island, and currently have Australia and beyond ahead. In summary, we have circumnavigated the Atlantic, crossed the Pacific, and now have the Indian Ocean in helm.

We choose this life of high highs and low lows. There are very few in-betweens, and if there are, the call to head out creeps back into the soul within a week. I can be covered in puke, holding a bucket for one of my children or me, pushed all around by waves and wind, trying to cook on a gimbaled stove, and curse the life, but once we hit land, and discover a new place and culture, within a week, we are all saying, "What's next!?" The life can also be filled with calm seas and a perfect wind, whales following with their songs echoing through the hull, my soul filled to the brim with gratefulness and awe. Like I mentioned, high highs and low lows.

We sail because we can. Nick survived the storm that hit the Chicago to Mac race on Lake Michigan in 2011. The sky turned green with lightning, the rail was in the water with no sail, and the wind blew to 110 knots. I said, "If you can do that and get home safely, I trust you." Sure, it can be terrifying, and I can hold my youngest child in my arms, feel *Selkie* sliding down gigantic waves, see my husband white-knuckle the helm, and curse my choices, but I can also be sailing downwind on a sunny day surrounded by hundreds of dolphins as far as the eye can see. I can slowly slide over a dark, night sea that has rivers of glowing jellyfish. I can dip my hands into the ocean after the sunsets with my oldest son and play with the phosphorescence like we have magic wands. I can be fully dressed in my bibs, jacket, and hat and be pounding into the waves taking on water, watching schoolbooks float on the floor, and pray for the sun to rise, but I can also be moored outside the Pitons on Christmas and venture inland for a mud bath and a rinse in the natural pools. I can be tied to a dock banging and banging in strong winds knowing that something might break and that it's unsafe to leave the boat, or I can be tied to a dock under a castle in Scotland talking to locals about life on the sea. I can be motoring through a billion jellyfish but be in the middle of a fjord watching cliff jumpers parachute down around me. Why do I sail? I'm addicted to these high highs and low lows. The more I see of the world, the more I realize there is so much more to see.

A sturdy anchor hold, a cityscape, a distant island, cobalt water moving in a steady breeze that fills my sails, a child in my arms who smells like salt, a single pelican, a tangerine sunset–these enchant me. Forty-nine feet of hull filled to the brim with my husband and four children is magical. When I share this and write, I am usually under the vastness of an immense number of stars, Milky Way brilliant, moon a sliver, phosphorescence in the water, waves sliding under in darkness, sails staying full, waves lapping with kindness, hot tea cupped in hand, words chosen carefully for a poem—these are my perfect night moves on the ocean. When things are all just right, there is quiet, creativity, a simile, a juxtaposition.

Sometimes things aren't perfect. Most frequently we are asked, "What is the worst weather you have ever seen?" There are six answers in six years: storm mid-north Atlantic with no help in sight, against wind and tide coming out of the Kiel Canal, psychologically finished off the shores of Portugal, petrified that the nine fishing boats surrounding us around Honduras were pirates, the Skagerrak above Denmark, and hitting a convergence zone between Bora Bora and Tonga, which resulted in needing to take sanctuary inside Beveridge Reef.

Of course, it is interesting to tell these stories, but what I find more enchanting is a regular day. When the air is right, the coffee is made, and no one is seasick, schoolbooks come out. On a weekday at sea, Wi-Fi does not exist. We have loads of books piled high under the foot of our bed in the aft, lined up on floors in bags, and completely covering the foot space on my side of the bed for the entire school year. This particular year, these books were accumulated in the States, packed in bags, hauled through airports, brought from rental to rental in the Yucatán on scuba adventures, and then finally delivered to the boat to successfully prepare for a school year, or a similar situation during a different year. My older two kids, a sophomore in high school and a middle schooler, do school in their own time, in their own way, only asking for help when they need it, and when it is time for me to go over it. I spend the rest of the day schooling my first and fourth grader until the day is almost done. It's usually tied in with cooking and cleaning, sailing and singing, but mostly involves what other kids their age are doing in desks in stable rooms all over the world. One that does not move with the sway of the waves. I also try to weasel in my graduate work with any free time I have, either getting a daily dose of reading done or whittling away at a paper. Only if I'm extremely lucky on the weekends do I find time to do what I love, which is to write.

Magic mostly occurs when we are at sea, and I am awakened for my night shift around 2:00 or 3:00 in the morning. The water world looms, and the stars spill in the skies with as much mystery as the water below. No boat in sight, just pure water, wind, and our floating home in movement with the earth's elements. I'm alone. My family sleeps, and I have my tiny phone to write a poem. The top hatch of the hard Bimini is pushed wide open, and strapped into the cockpit with my life jacket, I poke my head out by the sails to locate all the constellations and planets I know. Mystical enchantment is an understatement. It is vast bewilderment, awe of circumstance, humbleness in survival. The night sky splits open for me like a river, and the breeze opens and satisfies my soul. I am completely within myself—alive. Anything could happen, yet there is a notion that this current situation will hold, and I may just be held in it. There is so much unseen space that could possibly swallow me, but for some reason comforts me, and I am not lonely. Rain could sprinkle, stars could dwindle, but the phosphorescent sea that leaves behind fairy dust will twinkle brighter. The sea salt in the air splashing from the break of waves on the hull softens my skin and my composure to love the life. The mud is washed away. No shoes needed. I've been to places and nestled my children near crocodiles, volcano eruptions, and turtles. I've kissed them to bed near giant reefs, coconuts, and to the rhythm of local music. We've lived through being stuck going back and forth, and now we leave whispers on the wind as we set out into what may seem like an endless horizon. The moon and its phases have filled our nights with stories. Full sails pulling us into darkness and the unknown has given us our bedtime lullabies. The breeze coming off the ocean is wrapped on me like a scarf, and the path that is laid out reflects light, a gift of the moon. The smile that creeps onto my face involves pre-dawn sea secrets that I try to hold fast within my aquamarine eyes. We have floated through the doorway into a protected place of non-stop wonder that contains musical giggles of children freed. The ocean life cares for me like a slow dance on my father's feet when I was young. I give up any control—I am spun. The repetition of the waves is my consistent heartbeat.

PART I

Moon Spotlight

Ocean of Storms

Poetry & Prose from Bora Bora to Tonga

Bora Bora to Tonga During Cyclone Season with a Leukemia Longitude

We are at sea again, with the *creak* of the boat and the *thromp* of the main. Memories of Bora Bora, Bloody Mary's Bar and Grill, and the full lunar eclipse on Halloween are on my mind, as we sway with the whistling wind. Like an eerie movie, the reflection of light lends the clouds a backlight. It is 1221 miles to Tonga. A squall simmers to starboard.

My family (four children, my husband and I) take the leap, again, leaving the comfort of land behind and risking an open ocean crossing to be somewhere new on our Westerly 49, *Selkie*.

The Cooks and Samoas are not an option during cyclone season. We must move on. Our plan is to finish the Pacific in New Zealand via Tonga. The first leg to Tonga, is predicted to be a slow journey. The ocean should treat us gently to start, then abruptly awaken on day eight. South winds should rise to meet us the last few days. At least, this is what is predicted. Our ship holds tightly to the sails like a tall tree to its branches that blow in the wind. This tale has a twist.

Our family had previously been sailing in the "correct" season to finish a Pacific Crossing (to get to New Zealand before November); however, during a short trip home from Tahiti, my brother was diagnosed with Leukemia, and I was a perfect (100%) match for a blood stem cell donation, which could save his life. Rather than returning to the Pacific in August, we arrived back in October. The possibility of saving my brother's life was the only thing that mattered. The price of our late departure was a more complicated sail. Worth it, but still difficult as we struggled to keep all of us alive in the South Pacific during cyclone season.

We waited out a storm in Moorea, then another in Bora Bora, before we found (with PredictWind—the app, and MetBob—a weather guru out of Auckland) that it was okay to start the first leg of the journey to Tonga and wait there before continuing onto New Zealand. The planned ten-day crossing was due to spin up some weather for the second half.

The first couple of days went smoothly. In my imagination, I pondered waves, scales, spikes, and monsters for pure entertainment. I enjoyed the breeze and sail and made sure my children were well fed and doing their schoolwork. But the wind and waves came early.

Slowly the wind and waves grew. If wind and waves pause or reach a plateau, they are mostly enjoyable, but these built and built before the forecasts had warned. They were supposed to come on day eight, and it was day five. I knew it was going to get worse. We pulled in the head sail, brought out the stay, and kept the main reefed.

The Pacific tossed us and tossed us at night, especially in the dark. I slept with Rory (6) and Mara (9), in the aft. We slept sideways in bed to attempt to handle the heeling combined with the jolting. Every third wave would send my arms out to clutch my sleeping children. A small struggle played on their faces, and I apologized to them in my mind. The rail dipped and we slept standing for a moment and fell back down. I watched them breathe and tried to breathe myself. I'm not good with this kind of anxiety. We have been a live-aboard sailing family for almost six years. You'd think I would know better by now? *Hold*, I whispered to myself. *This could be a nightmare. Hold,* Selkie, *hold.*

Fear, anger, sadness due to the sea state and lack of control made me want to scream, "Don't go to the South Pacific!" to other sailors, but no one could hear me. I tried to channel bravery, to rise above the *slam, splash, whoosh, whirl*, and found myself praying to Mother Earth. It's a Conversion Zone. It looks blue and peaceful on PredictWind, but it is anything but peaceful. It's a place that wants to swallow boats. A confused sea that would be fine enfolding any sailor into the depths. *Slip, slap, sink, sunk, just like that,* I thought, and my morale floated down to the bottom silt. I thought of my brother on chemo, and I knew we were both battling to live. Oh, but my husband, the captain, and all my children were fine. The youngest would even shout, "Wee," occasionally.

"If Dad's okay, we're okay, Mom," my eldest son, Tristan (16) said coolly and calmly. My eldest daughter, Lily (14), put in her earbuds and turned her face to the sea and wind. She was cool with it too. My eyes bugged out of my head, as I looked behind her and saw the waves coming one after another after another with no sign of sitting down. The sea was like a lioness: ready, biding her time, waiting for the perfect moment to pounce. I felt her crouching, teaching her cubs, the small squalls, to surround us. She was teaching them to hunt us, us sailors trying sweetly to pass by.

With this wind and waves came unimaginable speed. Our sailing vessel is comfortable with 4-8 knots, but we were going 10-12. It felt like an unstoppable train. At night, this train sped into darkness. The waves stole my breath, pulled at my ribs, and made my heart skip. Every second was absorbing bounces, stretches, pulls. There was nothingness and everything: stars, bottomless wonder. We were being pulled, stretched, with the ocean at the helm. *I surrender*, I whisper to myself. I must not worry. It is not good for morale. I must trust in my life choices, my husband, our ship. Our children have been trained and raised to this life. *Breathe.*

Finally, something happened in my favor. We got notice of a Hail Mary from MetBob. Two other boats were doing the journey as well. Beveridge Reef, an atoll only allowed to be used by sailors during emergencies off Niue, was nearby. We turned to port.

A day out from the reef, we discovered that the whisker pole for the stay sail was broken due to pressure. Nick took it down and we rolled it in. More squalls and rain came and went. We tried to dodge them like coconuts falling from a tree, but we had to make it to the reef before dark. The ocean continued to dish out huge waves, but the wind started to calm down for a bit. We had to turn off course for a while to take the waves off the beam and put them behind us. It got rough, and Nick sent Tristan out to change the boom preventer from mid-boom to the end of the boom to correctly place it. If the boom pulled to starboard side and dipped in the water, it could have been cracked. Everyone kept an eye on the barometer to prepare for more changes.

We saw floating mast lights before we saw any sliver of sand, and that's what it was—almost completely submerged, an otherworldly sanctuary in the middle of the Pacific. We made it through the pass, dropped the anchor, floated the chain, and cooked a good meal (white fish with grapefruit, coconut rice, and zucchini). It was loved, and immediately we all slept through the night. Eight days at sea. Two to go. We waited.

The wind whistled through us in the night, and we pulled ungodly hard on our anchor. Even though the boat was lateral, it felt vertical like we were a hanging time piece on the world's edge. The coral reefs were like small stitches holding us dangling in the pocket of the ocean. The waves were dissipated by the reef, and we had a moment to collect our thoughts and sea-weathered souls back into brave sailors again, or at least, I did.

The next day the worst wind whistled, and we were happy not to be in the open. Rested, at night under the stars, we gathered on the bow, the wind whipped our hair, and the jellyfish lit up like magic wee clusters spewing dust spells, nymph-like, and I was tenderized into the mystery and endless wonder of the ocean again—content, thankful, grateful. Most importantly, I knew my brother was getting my stem cell transplant back in Michigan, and he was to begin his restart on life. I was calmed.

The last two days, the Pacific was sleeping as we moved to Tonga. Our code zero bulbed, there was a vermillion sunrise, and I said, *Shh, Ocean, shh. Stay asleep. May sweet witches keep you under a spell.*

This crossing rattled me to the core. There were many tears shed—only by me. It wasn't the first time, and it won't be the last. We had the second leg to New Zealand approaching. That is another story, and I am going to pick a better weather window to tell it.

Moon Spotlight

The clouds and squalls block most of the light,
so she fights to glare down with a spotlight
on the water. The Pacific answers back
through the dark with suspense. Sunrise—
tangerine, turns my head, back at the surface
the depths are rising too late to finish ascent.
I peer over the edge and watch them sink
to try again tomorrow. Scales, spikes, tongues
breathe in the salt patiently for the proper occasion.

255 Degrees

we turn towards Tonga,
wing to wing, moon and mars
swell from the south sway,
i cried before bed, not knowing
where i belong, my girls sleep
in my bed, my eldest son sails,
my husband on watch teaching,
my youngest, now six, says, space,
he's too big to cuddle his mom,
my husband cries too, missing
his dad, it's a strange space,
the ocean, tossing, testing,
releasing, growing, i wake
not knowing where i am,
sloppy anchorage, really rollie,
into the cockpit for my watch,
plain and simple, normal
by day three, the air is clear,
like the water is dark, like stars
are apparent, sail straight,
south route, near south pacific
cyclones, hoping to sneak gently
west, so much water, so much
mystery, i lie on my back, barefoot,
playing with winches, cranks,
mechanisms in my toes, lives
in my hands, wind my only friend.

Darkness Patches the Moonlit Sky

Guess it's my turn. Tossing and turning in bed is getting me nowhere anyway. I think I've woken up like every ten minutes.

I wiggle out of the sheets between two sleeping children, one cuddling a unicorn and the other a hairy cow. I tuck them back in and shiver.

Rory, here is Harry, your hairy cow. Mara, here is Lucky, your unicorn. Tuck. Tuck. Brr. It's cold. Nothing to stop the wind.

Grab the railing! A random wave pushes me. *Get your ocean balance, Maggie. Argh. Embarrassing. At least no one was here with their eyes open to see.*

Should I change? Nope. My pajama dress will stay on because it holds remnants of warmth. Too cold. Where are those thermal leggings that I haven't used since Scotland. Ah. There they are. Ew. They stink. Must be moldy. Oh well. I'm cold. Shimmy those on. Try not to fall over. Sweater too. And my hat. Where's my favorite knit hat? Mmm. Good. Like capping a good wine and saving it for later. That's me.

Pushing up on my toes, I peer out the hatch.

My Westerly 49, Selkie, *was definitely built for a taller version of me. It must have been built for tall gents. There's that weird British accent sneaking in my head again. She's made in England. Not all the English are tall. Accommodations. Gotta accommodate. Can't make small boats and assume tall men would like to lean over all day. Not all sailors are tall. I'm jealous of the view a few more inches would give me. But…*

Endless stars. Endless ocean. Yep. Still here. Middle of the Pacific.

Wild waves. Such wild waves. Inches from the hatch, but still not likely to come in. Should I close them? No. It gets so stuffy down here for the kids, my four brave kids.

Through the galley, the food wrappers reveal how my husband has kept himself awake: coffee bag, tea bags, chips, gummies, lollipops, and orange peels. *He must have been bored. Seems a bit rough out there to be bored.*

Whoop. Hang on. That's a big one.

A huge wave hits, the gimbaled stove rears sideways, and I catch the coffee pot before it falls. *Thank the gods, it's not hot!* A deep aroma of espresso fills my mouth and lungs, as I wipe the end of the leftover brew from my hand. *Still smells good.*

Okay. Let's see what we've got.

I turn the bend, from the red-lit saloon, hold the railing to the stairs, and take in the sight of my husband on watch. Instruments and computers give a romantic, blue-contrasted light. *Come on, old girl, you got this.*

Four steps, and, *plunk*, my ass goes down. *Won't move for a bit now. I'm a bit grumpy. Gotta wake up.*

He smiles at me. Smiles. Humph. Gotta wake up.

"So… How was it?" I ask. My voice finally leaves my brain to interact. *Good for me. Some human interaction. Not all elementals. Wind. Water. Human. My human.*

Why was he using my computer? Careful! Give it to me. All my graduate work on one device! My life in there. Ahh. Safe in my arms.

He zooms in on the nav and looks behind the helm.

"I was about to wake you up. The squalls have passed. I think it's easy sailing for a bit."

"Just the way I like it."

"Been pointed at about 255 degrees, trying to work up to 265, but it won't stick. Either will be okay. Still got, what, seven days to go, right? What day is it?"

"Night three. Thursday." *Try not to roll your eyes, Maggie. Whew. Grumpy. Sailors aren't supposed to know what day it is. I do. As a student. As a teacher. I need to know. Guess I'm not a complete sailor? Hmph. Gotta cheer up.*

"I tried to wake you earlier. Squeezed your hand. All you did was smile and keep sleeping."

"Ha. Haha." I laugh. The dark grumpiness beginning to crumble off me. *Oh, that feels good.*

"There is not much wind, and not much moon," he says.

I peer around the night sky looking for my night light, the moon. The only light that doesn't send us plummeting into complete darkness. *Where are you? Nope. Nothing. So dark. So dark.*

"Depending on the instruments then?"

"Yep. Except the radar keeps going out."

He descends the stairs to fiddle with the gauges, turning them on and off, hoping for a different result.

I have a moment to crumble more of my grumpy exterior. I slide into a life jacket, strap in, and peer over the side. In the dark, when there is no moon, the vast mysteries of what's underneath show a little glimmer. The bioluminescent plankton sprays off the sides of our hull, as we slide over the ocean's surface. *And yep, there goes the rest of my grumpy exterior. Acclimation, baby.*

"There ya go. Some radar for now. No squalls. Wing to wing is working well."

Let me check that scenario. I stand on the bench in the cockpit, push my head through the hatch, and take in the main sail pushed to one side, and the head sail full on the other. Wing to wing. Selkie *in her ghost moth stage. This builds a cheerier exoskeleton. Move over clouds.*

Smooch. Squeeze. A kiss and a touch of hands, and he is gone into the darkness of the bumpy v-birth.

Settle. Sigh. Write a poem.
It's a small poem tonight. Straight and to the point of the endless expanse of our water planet and how hard a night shift can be. I like it.

I look over my star app and find the constellations that I can around the patches of clouds. *Just me and stars, and ocean, and wind, and possible dangers.* I think on my family and friends back in the States and other countries in beds that don't move. *No night shift required for them. Sigh. Appreciate it, Maggie. Love the space you have chosen.*

The wind picks up on port side. Instead of heading off course, I pull in the main. *Crank. Crank. Gotta do more push ups. My arms are weak.* Loosen high side. Prep low side. *Turn helm. Turn. Tack. Pull. Pull. Crank. Crank. Lock her down.*

Nice broad reach.

Tonga still in my sights. Wind. *Wind? Stay calm. Stay calm.*

Time for *my* coffee.

Looming

The wave. The squall. The rain. The wind.
Vast ocean. Starless sky.

Me. Estranged. Alone. Floating.
Riding. Writing. — To Be.

Sea of Clouds

When I pretend
you are here,
my tongue
and lips
spill stories

wing to wing
my sails match
puffy white
clouds blending
into oblivion
like a night moth

Let the wind
whistle,
drop
the anchor,
write only a moment

Black and white
the night
glimmers on ocean
moon reflection
sail and rail

all shades of grey

like a photo
from the past
I am alone

photographer
unseen

Limits of Trust

Tonga pulls your heart—leaving pieces behind. A wave
like that scratches the limits of trust. This wave, the one
that makes me breathe deeper, or that wave, the one
that steals from my ribs. Speed. Full head, full stay, full
main sail—racing. Tied to fabric with stretched stitches.
Racing. Cutting waves. Time is every second absorbed
into these bounces, sways, stretches, pulls. Nothingness
and everything, stars and bottomless wonder. Pull stretch,
racing. The ocean hums me along. I completely surrender.

3 * Starlights

bobbing
anchor
lights
under a dark looming
sky
keep us company
strangers
companions of emergency
then
my lanky, lean, teenage son
night
dives in darkness, whipping
wind
my daughter watches him jade
on her neck
from Guatemala
jelly fish light, magic wee clusters
spewing
dust water spells like nymphs
gloom
darkness
cyclone
fear
tenderizes me into ocean
mystery
love
endless
wonder

no wind

nothing but
a black eery
lagoon spilling
lost at sea
saying
forgotten
only me
and my
milkyway
following into
jupiter's light
billions
of bursting
fiery stars
mars crowns
taurus
my zodiac
positioned
between
the pointed
horns
like a flower
growing
near danger
i will braid
my hair for
tennyson
to wear
pleiades
like fireflies
aldebaran
will replace
my right eye

to look at me
twill be hard
to look
away
here
in nowhere
where
my soul
belongs
home
away
from chaos
standing
stretching
knowing
i belong
where
slow
moves
otherworld
doorways
selkies
sirens
banshees
hold
my hand
doldrums
paint
my skin
midnight
possibilities
and space
dress me
in endless
ocean

the fabric
rippling
swelling
absorbing
the labyrinth
of time

Sea of Fertility:
Poetry & Prose from Tonga

A Moth in the Darkness

brings Mandy Haggith's secrets on wing whispers.
The spill of the moonlight calls me and disappears.
A broch, a forest, a loch, a sea, I am with her—
west coast Scotland, Assynt, finger into the sea.
Her worry on paper, polar bears, history, climate
recycles in my soul keeping me from my coffin.
I take a deep breath. The ocean tickles the shore
in my ears circling me to stones, sand, coconuts.
Bobbing at anchor near Ovaka, Vava'u, Tonga,
a kingdom never colonized, kept to itself, filled
with expats. There is food in my fridge, fruit
hanging from the nets, sleeping children below.
I think of the young woman who offered herself
to my husband at the grocery, and reflect
on what paradise means to her. A cloud covers
the moon as it would during the Iron Age, current
age, post-apocalyptic age, and a giant, dark moth
traps itself in my cockpit, fluttering and hitting
itself against the walls and window when there
are so many openings. I toss a light towards aft
to guide it back into a starless night, a vast ocean.
Its wings continue to flutter calling meal to birds.
Strangeness is here on the water now, enjoying
me by myself—licking its lips—thirsty for words.

"Do coconuts grow when you pick them out of the ocean and throw them into the nearby brush?" I asked myself. My toes lapped in the water, and I tried not to curse the world for all the plastic garbage along the shore of the deserted island in Vava'u, Tonga. "Of course, they will!" I said to the sea with an imaginary pat on my back to erase apocalyptic thoughts of humanity. I imagine big trees oxygenating the world because of this beach walk crossing my fingers.

To recycle my soul through the debris, I wade in, watch little white fish scatter their school, and clutch another. "Whew, you're a heavy, big boy. I throw you for the next generation!" I laugh as my toss results in barely any distance from the water's edge.

"Ovaka," I whisper the name of the island and most likely pronounce it wrong. "Ovaka," again. No response from the sea. It talks to itself—back and forth, back and forth having the same conversation. The trash says nothing, but I can feel my eyes turn blood red as I stare at it—my eyes turning into incinerators.

My mind wanders to the young woman who offered herself to my husband at the grocery store yesterday. Her body gleaming with perfect island skin, long dark curly hair, and hopeful eyes. My husband with his red hair (going salt n'pepper), skin freckled with possible ocean sun damage, and his understanding smile. "Um, no. No, thank you, but if…" he said. He told me the story before bed, and I could picture it all in my head.

She responded with a "But if? Later then? I can be your girlfriend? Your wife?"

I picture the store more in my mind, and I can see the back door swing open letting the sunlight pour in. A starved dog covered in flies rests chained to a building brick. Her nipples sore and stretched from her recent litter. The American top hits played too loudly for shoppers inviting such an eager party atmosphere to groceries. The smell of freshly baked bread for sale mixed with the sensation of the liquor bottles that gleamed in the sun.

A friend of the grocery girl peaked her head around the end corner of the aisle giggling to see if he would accept. *I'm sure that made it more awkward. Maybe more tempting?*

He blushed. Mouth dry. Hard to speak. "No. I meant. If I wasn't… I mean… You are pretty." He paused.

"But is she here?" and she dared to reach out and put her hand on his as she asked about me. *About me. Me. And touched him.* A bit of a language barrier. He had told me, *but it didn't seem like they had much of a language barrier to me.* All those walls could have come down easily.

"Wife. Happy." He looked at his list in my writing to move his hand away. "Just a trash bag please." He pointed at his tattooed ring finger with a compass pointing north. *Was I still his north? I guess he proved himself.*

I wade in. The little white fish scatter again. I clutch another coconut and chuck it in the brush. *What is paradise to her? Definitely not this.* I frown at all the garbage, and a huge, plastic fender to a sailboat. *Someone's probably missing that. Not her. Not her. Not the girl in the aisle at the grocery.*

I think on the giant moth last night hitting herself over and over again in the cockpit's hard Bimini glass, when she had so many other ways to get out. I still feel the solar light in my hand, as I tossed it out of the cockpit and watched the moth follow it into the darkness of the Pacific. I grab another coconut from the small-pebbled sand that sticks to my ankles in such weird ways—making me statuesque. *Humph.* It thuds hard and rolls.

My toes pinch back into my fins, my face back into my goggles, and my lungs back into a snorkel tube. *I'm taking this fender with me! I'll put it to good use. Recycle. Reuse.*

The line of it hurts my fingers as I pull and swim the long length back to *Selkie*, my Westerly 49, my home with my husband and four kids. *We squeeze well.*

I think I'll name this fender, Bob. He scratches my fingers again in approval. *That will make my kids laugh and welcome him aboard.*

Swim. Swim. No coral. No coral. Still no coral. Ooo! A patch of coral! I desert Bob the fender with a deep breath and swim down a few meters for a closer look at the families of fish. *The blue ones. With black. Yes. They're my favorite.* Lungs tighten. Back up I go. Hand back on Bob's fender line.

No coral. No coral. Swim. No coral. Only one patch of coral in this long stretch! What the fuck! Fuck! Fuck. The world is ending. No one takes care of the water. Breathe, Maggie, breathe.

My fingers find the ladder, and I throw the fender on the aft.

"Kids! Hey, guys! Come meet Bob!"

Tongan Naiads

island with the half-bare tree swings
protected by nymph-like nude visits
this sandy beach swallows curious feet
perfect shell scatters tiny crab skitter
squid and jelly stings on kicking legs
the coral fish families protect their young
caves swallow fruit bats to taste the dark
sleeplessness calls a shooting star to fall
a papaya drops with a thud and goes silent
pineapple ants devour a succulent break
sway them like a floating art piece satisfied
they have buried my heart in cerulean coral
hold my hands as they submerge
attempt to follow tongan naiads deep

Crevices and Coconuts

When the light through the water webs
on the bottom of the sea. Catch me.

When the black-winged butterflies fly
into crevices of mangroves. Comfort me.

When the coconut washes ashore harry
looking to root in shade. Plant me.

When the small fish is curious in my curves
around my bathing suit and legs. Love me.

When the letter bends, stands tall, circles,
dots, zigzags into poetic words. Write me.

Poverty & Paradise

Bile rises in the stomach like a jellyfish
hungry
sting
I'm sitting with you again in a new
tropical
paradise
Waitress uniforms, starched, ignoring
crawling
roaches
Ashamed. I reach out. A hug. Our he/she
waitress that meets me in the streets
calls me by name. Knowing my name. My
voice. Her strong, Tongan figure. I thank
the world for him/her multiple times. How
sweet. How rough. How real the life
of food. We've
eaten enough
for takeaway
I offer an apple to the girl who stares
the boy in rags
the banana lady
who *gives me* extra

Rocky, Blue Coral Wonders

When we navigate the place that you should not go,

past the markings that do not exist, through and by

light patches of rocky coral, down and past through

dark blue where we see the Pacific Ocean explode

on the rocks, drop the anchor, send the kids ashore.

It is time for just you and me, the sea caressing shell.

Sea of Nectar:

Poetry & Prose from Tonga to New Zealand

Chased by Santa at Sea:
The Sailing Journal & Poetry of a Busy Mom

December. We float on a mooring ball, downtown Neiafu, Vavau, Tonga, deep in the Pacific Ocean. Our two youngest, Rory (6) and Mara (9), wipe their sleeping eyes to rise and open another day of their advent calendar, and then check on what mischief Elf on the Shelf, Buddy, has gotten into during the night. He has crawled into Mara's stocking hanging in the saloon and thrown his raincoat outfit around the few presents we've been able to find, purchase, and wrap. Tonga is extremely scarce when looking for Christmas presents or food. Nonetheless, a day of errands is in the works, if we want to leave for New Zealand tomorrow. With seven souls aboard, my husband (Nick), our two teenagers (Tristan and Lily), our littles (Mara and Rory), and Emma (our boat hitchhiker), we have all squeezed into 49 feet on our Westerly, *Selkie*, since before Thanksgiving (about a month now). We have prepared time and time again, stocking the boat with two weeks of food, only to be thwarted by an incoming storm. This will be our third attempt in three weeks.

A new kid boat is here, *Rainbow Safari*, with four kids, which started in Singapore, and are headed in the opposite direction than us. Since Covid, Tonga has only recently opened back up. We were the seventh boat allowed in after three years. We have a play date planned after lunch with their kids by dinghy.

I go to town with Emma and Mara. We do a little shopping, and then some provisioning. We must borrow money from Emma to do so, because the ATMs are down again, and she has cash. I grab the laundry, done by the local coffee shop, and Emma stays for the WIFI. Mara and I head back. I unpack, cook lunch, then take the kids to *Rainbow Safari* for their playdate. They stay there all day with their iPads, swimsuits, crafts, and toys. I go back to town for more provisions. Emma catches up and helps. Mostly it is secret present shopping. Back to *Selkie*, currently squeezing in all seven of us eager humans during the holidays. Then of course, I have more unpacking to do. Always a need to find a new place for storage: back of closet, under floorboards, underbeds, in bags in plain sight, and all cupboards filled to the brim. I get a migraine. I try to rid myself of it with a lot of water and a swim—nope. Nap.

Nick is off to check us out of customs with Emma. Our weather window is moved up a day. It works. All checked out. Kids return. Lily stays alone on the boat, which she likes to do to actually get some alone time. The rest of us go to one last dinner at the *Kracken*. Emma takes some photos, and *Rainbow Safari* comes to join us. We get to know yet another kid boat that we will never know when we will see again. They are adventurous and kind. I get to know our waitress more, we've been coming here a lot, so I kind of already know her well, but this time I ask about her family. Born and raised in Tonga, she loves it, and she is happy with her job. We stay till bedtime, 9 o'clock, and dingy back to *Selkie* in the dark. Straight to tucks and bedtime. We should get an early start tomorrow.

Sunday. Departure day. Still on a mooring ball, downtown Neiafu, Vavau, Tonga, deep in the Pacific Ocean. We sleep in but not without radio interference and Lily's alarm. Then it's up and to work for departure. I fix my ethics application for my dissertation. This is my third and final year finishing my 2nd masters. This one will be a MLitt in Highlands and Islands Literature based in Orkney. It's been my way of keeping Scotland with me since we sailed away from there in 2019. It's my favorite place in the world. Currently, the other side of the world.

Nick and Tristan are on cleaning and fix-up projects. Lily comes with Emma and me to the deli. They are expats that live in Tonga that prepare food for sailors. It's really the only way to get semi-decent food on the island. They are not ready. Twenty minutes of talking, baking, and bagging and we say goodbye. Back to *Selkie*.

The little girl from *Rainbow Safari* comes over to play with Rory after their swim. I unpack and serve up a lot of baguettes. Then I cook up leftovers and clean up. *Rainbow Safari* comes to get their little miss, and we wave goodbye as we drop the line from the mooring ball and motor out in high spirits.

As soon as we get to the ocean, Nick notices a dime-size tear in the main. We pull it down, I stitch it with the fishbone technique, and then we pull it back up. Nick is doing a lot of talking to teach Emma. I feel like she doesn't want to learn from me, so I keep it to a minimum, but I could be wrong. Our Code Zero, our light-wind sail, goes up, big and deep purple, and we are moving, no racing towards New Zealand!

Sooner than expected there is too much wind for the Code Zero, so we take it back down. Regular head sail out. Charging motor but sailing 6 knots in 11 knots of wind. I go over Lily's schoolwork. There is a lot of snacking: baguettes, cheese, cucumbers, and Emma's market fruit (soursop). Nick goes down for a nap. Tristan is at the helm with Lily and Emma lying about. I go over school with Tristan in the cockpit, while we talk with Emma on sailing and hash out cool *Macbeth* stuff for my dissertation.

Rory does some crafts. Mara explores the New Zealand guidebook that I have read and marked up cover to cover. Tristan takes off autopilot and sails by hand. Lily keeps sleeping. Daddy too. Sweet and sour chicken is admired, while I cook, and delicious to eat together in the cockpit. Much talk occurs, and it is a good time. Tristan does the dishes.

I listen to music and write a poem. Emma and Nick have a talk on her ex-boyfriends. All cleaned up for the first nightshift. I take the littles to the aft to sleep. Emma and Lily go to the v-birth. Nick and T get the first two nightshifts, and I listen to them quote movies and laugh on the open ocean. I write a poem, "Reflection." Day one done. Nine to go.

Reflection

there I am
in the ripples
turning into
burning coal orange
cobalt stealing-soul blue
curious oblivious gray
creeping soaring midnight
the last of me
floating on pacific
an inch above
keeping mystery
below

Monday

Day two. At sea between Tonga and New Zealand deep in the Pacific Ocean. Tristan wakes me at 3 am. We are super close to the group of islands, Ha'apai, two and a half miles close! They are good protection though. The night is calm, and the sail is sweet. Lily gets up and talks with me for over an hour. I write a poem, "Ha'apai," and watch the sunrise. Emma gets up on her own, and we talk on religion and upbringing. I make a breakfast taco. Coffee is on, and Nick is up. He joins us.

Rory has been up for a while, so I feed Nick and Rory some cereal. I lay in the aft and do math and phonics with my two younger children. Our snack time is more baguettes. I take a nap. Second snack is cucumbers. Emma likes hers with salt. Emma, Lily, and Mara begin to feel seasick. I study the forces of nature for science with Mara. Nick has been fixing broken things all morning, Tristan goes up the mast to look at the radar. Lunch is to order—sandwiches, spaghetti, ramen—all cooked up. Emma doesn't feel well. I give her a seasick patch, and she mostly sits on the couch watching shows.

I clean up and take a nap. Not a very long one though. I'm back up doing school with Mara and Rory. Then I must take another nap. Teens wait till late in the day to do school. Lily is seasick, so she does a half day. Tristan likes to do his on watch in the cockpit. Code Zero is up, and we are in a fast current. In 13 knots, we go 8! Nick naps. I go over mountain hikes with Tristan that we hope to accomplish in New Zealand. We circle them all on the map, and I do more reading of the New Zealand guidebook for fun. We start Rory's "sensible" party for his science with everyone trying to write their senses on sailing down on paper. We wake Nick and hand out stuffed animals for comfort that represent each person on board, which gives us all a laugh. Nick wins the writing award due to the word Valhalla in his sense paragraph. He knew how to play it up for the boys. Nick eats up his glory. He loves winning. Then I help Lily with her algebra, and parent the youngest two during their meltdowns.

Dinner is BBQ pork sandwiches with veggies, fries, leftovers, and nuggets. Rory has three sandwiches! Everyone gets plenty full. Mara has a meltdown realizing that Christmas will be at sea. I let her cry, then cheer her up. "Santa will find us and come down the mast instead of a chimney!" We play the word game with pictures, then tuck into bed as early as we can. After I make them laugh really hard about the Christmas lights in the head, the bathroom, being a "toilet-tree," they will never forget—best Xmas ever! Nick and T are on the first two night-shifts again.

Ha'apai

looks close in the dark
under the moon as we
gently sail full canvas
to the west ocean calm

Virgo misled us too close
calling hull to reef to sand
to Fotuhaa, Tofua, Kotu,
whispering stay with

whistling wind, friendly,
fluffy clouds, milky way
spill, I steer away looking
longingly knowing mystery

Scorpio joins me, questions
me, till comets stream long
with burning embers close
on the horizon igniting poetry

Tuesday

Day three. Still at sea between Tonga and New Zealand deep in the Pacific Ocean. I postpone my shift until 3:33 am and find Tristan on his computer, and Lily asleep in the cockpit in her mermaid blanket. Tristan goes to his bunk, and all but me sleep on. I look at the stars, stay on the rhumb line, write a poem, "Undersea Peak," text family, and veer around Ata Island. At 7 am, I make breakfast for myself and work on my computer for my dissertation. Emma is up watching shows again in the v-birth, Rory is on his iPad, and then the sun wakes Lily in the cockpit. Day on.

I do math and phonics with Mara and Rory in the aft, before I even feed them breakfast. Then I make sure everyone is fed who wants to be fed. I take some time to organize Rory's schoolwork, and take time to write postcards to all close friends and family. It makes me a bit seasick. I pep up and do a friction lesson with Mara that includes an experiment, then I'm on left-overs, ramen, and cucumbers for lunch by 11 am. I'm down by 1130 to study and nap. I do some forces of nature with Mara, then take a break with my New Zealand guidebook in the cockpit. We mostly talk with whomever is there. I persuade Mara to read *The Big Friendly Giant* (BFG) and finish her day of school. She does so willingly and thanks me—it's a nice change. Rory and Mara game. Nick naps. I go back to the cockpit to be on watch.

Nick wakes and talks to me about Jamie and Behan's opinion from *Sailing Totem*. They are a well-known sailing couple that helps sailors navigate at sea. Currently they are guiding us southeast as fast as we can to avoid a storm that is bearing down on us from the north. We knew it would. We must keep up speed, wind, or no wind. They tell us to go west to a current that will move us faster south. The storm to the north has sped up and is coming faster. We joke on how it must be Santa—chased by Santa at sea. We go west and wing to wing with pole support. This is when we hold the main to starboard, and we keep the head sail out to port. It resembles a butterfly. The boys have a hard time untangling the halyard for the code zero after the head sail is out. I find it very entertaining. I wish and hope that it is the most exciting thing that will happen the whole trip. I don't want that storm to catch us. It looked gnarly on our Windy App, before we left.

I make hotdogs with buns that are way too big, fries, and carrots. Still, everyone eats and asks for more dogs without buns. Pickles are sought after and fought over. Tristan does the dishes for the second time of the day. I wish Emma would help more, since we are giving her a free ride and free food. Nick and I get in a fight about motoring. He said we'd have enough fuel, but he lied. He said he didn't have enough time, but that's a lie too. I'm angry with him when I go to bed, but I still game with the littles and try to make them happy. Tristan and Nick are on the first two nightshifts again. Day three complete.

Undersea Peak

climbs from six thousand
to less than three hundred
and I have summited with
Selkie, my sailboat. Steep
crags needed no line. Bare-
foot with a southern current
up I drifted soaring reaching
the precipice eyewitness
of horizon to horizon in all
directions. I could touch
the moon, stand tall in her
spotlight, hold hands
with Chiron, the Centaur,
and his mother, Philyra,
the sea nymph. We breathe
in wind, harness latitude.

Wednesday

Day four. Still at sea between Tonga and New Zealand deep in the Pacific Ocean. Up just after 3:30 am for my shift. Tristan says to wake Daddy at the crack of dawn to put up the Code Zero. We are motor sailing, and the Pacific is being calm and nice to us. Mara wakes after a bug incident, and I put her on the couch—there are lingering cockroaches onboard, which are unavoidable bringing in food and tying up to islands near the equator. I write a poem, "Motor sailing," thinking about my fight with Nick the previous night, and try to meditate my way out of it. Then I am lucky enough to watch the crack of dawn appear on the horizon.

I wake Nick, we go to put up the Code Zero, but the halyard is tangled again, so we need to wake Tristan to take down the pole that holds it aloft. We work as a well-oiled machine quietly moving things into place during the dawn light. Rory wakes alone, and I put him in his room and make the bed for Nick. He goes back to sleep. Tristan stays up to study. I make us breakfast and dress for the day. We are going 9.4 knots in 10 knots. We must have found the southerly current that *Sailing Totem* recommended! Day on.

Lily wakes seasick. Nick gets up too. Mara opens the advent calendar and snuggles down. With Nick up, Rory demands that we put the bed back sideways in the aft. The way he likes it, so he doesn't fall out when heeling over. We do. I do math and phonics with the two littles. I hand out popsicles and go to take a nap. I ignore my own schoolwork. I get up and teach some forces of nature to Mara, and then I make leftover hot dogs and ramen. I get up and read some more of my New Zealand guidebook. It looks like such a wonderland of possibilities with good food. We haven't had healthy, good food in so long. Tonga had a problem with even getting fresh potatoes.

Nick and I work things out in the cockpit, then I finish school with the littles. I read some more of my guidebook, because I can't stop daydreaming about being on land with so many options. I've had quite a fill of deserted islands. We play a lot of music. I make nuggets, broccoli, and a Shepherd's pie—they are devoured. More music.

Nick and I argue about keeping the Code Zero up overnight. Couples at sea either work or don't. Thankfully, we are good at debating and working it out. We take it down after dark, due to my uncomfortable feeling that the wind will get too strong tonight. Up for sunset and to bed with the littles. During their nightshifts, Tristan and Nick sail through some lightning and squalls.

Motor Sailing

Moonrise. Cloudless.
Completely star-filled.

I try not to think on promises.
Meditate to the hum of motor.
Blank myself like black sea.
But history creeps in visible
like the dark side of moon.

It rises to stomach from spine,
which makes the walls ache
in this dark, limitless expanse
of time, nothingness, memories.

Moonrise. Perfection. A kind
smile. Forgiveness. Patience.
Love. Serenity. Misshapen
craters in a visibly perfect
circle. Embrace. Deepen.
Ponder. Appreciate invisible
moment like a dream brought
touchable, felt to skin, muscle
movement. I sail to keep up
with you, plan to merge
with you, take pictures
to keep you. Here where
ghosts steer, magic may
happen, and mystery finds
a rhythm on surface tension.

Thursday

Day five. Still at sea between Tonga and New Zealand deep in the Pacific Ocean. I take the shift from 3:30 am onwards. Tristan has a lot of instructions, but the night is simple with a motor sail and no squalls for me. Lily visits. I strap in and look at the stars, write a poem, "Tangled Lines," and finish the shift under the stars.

Nick wakes around 7, so I get Tristan up too. We try the Code Zero, and I go down for a nap. I wake to new instructions from *Sailing Totem* to keep up the speed, keep heading straight south for the east winds will pick up and be strong at the end. We do so. I make six loaves of bread. We eat five right out of the gate. Emma bounces around, but mostly watches shows. I do math and phonics with the littles. Tristan games with them and helps. Nick goes down for a nap.

I release Grandpa John, Grandma Mary, and Aunt Diana's mixed ashes. Ashes are not allowed to be brought into New Zealand. This day is the Winter Solstice, our Summer Solstice in the Southern Hemisphere. I release the dust into the ocean in hopes to keep their magic and protection with us. Tristan and Mara sew a hat with lots of instructions from Mara. I journal. The day is definitely on.

11 o'clock. I so don't want to do school, but I drag myself to the aft, and Mara and I get through forces of nature and her chapter book, *The BFG*, in one sitting, then Rory's schoolwork is to follow. The kids make a mighty mess in the aft to build a fort.

I settle and relax for a bit. I'm not needed to cook, clean, teach, study, or sail. That's rare. Tristan and Nick listen to a book in the cockpit. Then Tristan is on duty, while Nick naps, so I do spend some time outside helping, but then I'm back to my forced relaxation. I've gotta look after myself too. Later I make up a dinner of burgers, fruit salad, and cream corn rice. Some nuggets are added for Rory and Lily. I write a poem about slavery, then delete it, and cry on the floor—I think it's also due to my grandparents' ashes. The Pacific is not the Atlantic, but I dwell on the thought of being kept chained in the bottom of ship, stolen from my home, forced into a hideous future. I'm thankful for my freedom, and our ability to harness it with the wind.

I go to the bow for some time alone and some music. I write more poetry, "Winter Solstice." Tristan comes and asks to sew a sail for guppy from a towel. Of course! Then I go and watch River Dance with the littles before bed. We get halfway through and pass out. It's been a long day. Tristan and Nick deal with thunderstorms and no wind throughout their night-shifts. Day five done. Halfway!

Tangled Lines

Lightning in distance. Motor
sailing again. Time. Speed.
Needs to be maintained. Storm
after Christmas predicted. For now,

I strap into the stars. No moon
means every space in the night
sky, when your eyes adjust, becomes
a star. The mast stirs the Milky Way

spill. My daughter untangles lines,
the horizon stops flashing light,
and the hatches are pulled back
open to the ocean breeze. Behind

the helm, I watch the numbers, stay
the course. I ponder what it means
to be mysterious, to have secrets,
and my black nightgown holds to me

in the wet air, the stars fill my lungs,

and the deep sea infuses my bones

to turn my eyes a distant story blue.

Winter Solstice

The South
ern Hemi
sphere
is pure
day.

Wind slows.
We capture,
and I
drop

my ancestors' ashes:
Grandpa
John,
Grandma
Mary,
Aunt
Diana,

once owned
now spun.
Pacific
wind
snaps
again.

We

soar away.
I witness
the waves
dance
with
strong,
protective
crests.

Friday

Day six. At sea between Tonga and New Zealand deep in the Pacific Ocean. I'm up to do my shift, but Mara is scared. I cuddle her more, then get up and put the boys to bed. Nick goes in with the littles. There is rain and lightning. Thankfully hardly any thunder, so it is far off. I write a poem, "Glowing Birds," and watch the storm. A squall gives some wind, I pull out the sail, pull it back in, and out again. We motor mostly. Littles rise and so does Nick. I go to take a nap.

Mara divides presents and spreads them out all over the floor, so I'm up to make pancakes, with peaches, syrup, and powdered sugar! They are devoured and some are saved for sleeping Tristan. I have been wearing sweatshirts, but it is still warm enough to take it off. I do, but I make the littles wear clothes. They've been living in pajamas. Tristan is up and eats. I do math and phonics with Mara, and then Rory. I journal and work on poetry.

We motor on. The Code Zero needs to be taken down and unwrapped. It was done up too tightly in a squall. Nick lies on the dinghy on the bow, and Tristan works on it. I do some wrapping of presents for fun. Nick and I discuss how Emma fits with us in our family, but she is more like another kid than a nanny or sailor. Nick takes a nap. I do hobbies for Rory's school in the cockpit. We make leftovers, sandwiches, and ramen for lunch. Emma gets on dishes.

Mara wraps more presents. I finish school with Mara. We do fun balloon inertia and friction rocket experiments with bowling marbles too. We decide to gift our car crash experiment to Rory for Christmas, we read *BFG* and do the activities. Christmas break is on! No more school until New Zealand!

T and Nick listen to a book on audible. Emma and Lily go to their shows. We motor on. I play some app games, and then tend to the littles' hygiene by suiting them up in life jackets and cutting their nails into the ocean. Kids wrestle all over. I record some videos. We make homemade pizza, and Daddy and son are on for their nightshifts, and I am tucked in with the littles.

Glowing Birds

Lightning can be seen for miles.
It turns my vision on and off
like a scary movie, but the birds
from Raoul Island on Kermadec
Ridge land in the water, pick up
bioluminescence on their feet
and fly glowing around the boat.

Thunder is more terrifying—warning
of closeness. Our lightning rod
mast is alone out here calling
to the squall, teasing her. Darkness
is deep and we motor into it.

I didn't know it could get darker.

I believe in a clearing ahead, but
that seems to be an edge
that closes—too distant to reach.

The wet air is electric, streaks
crack the atmosphere, connect
ocean with sky. Go fast, *Selkie*.
Go faster. Water be frictionless.
Gravity ease up. Hull slice, move,
fly to a star-filled sky. Sides spill
phosphorescence helping us glow,
slide free. Windless, the storm lines
my port side—mouth open, thirsty.

Saturday

Day seven. CHRISTMAS EVE! Still at sea between Tonga and New Zealand deep in the Pacific Ocean. I'm awoken at 3:30 to Tristan and Nick turning off the motor to try the Code Zero. Nope. Back in. They head off to bed. There is no light, plenty of fog, and it is eerie quiet with no wind. We motor. I write two poems, "Hero" and "blank page," and imagine Santa shimming down the mast to deliver presents.

I wake Emma at 6 to do a shift, and I move Buddy, the elf on the shelf, and I as well must play the role of tooth fairy for Rory, before I tuck into bed with the littles again. I wake and the littles are quietly playing around me. I ask Rory, "What did the tooth fairy bring you?" He finds a pirate Lego to build and gets super excited. I help him build it a bit, then I'm up to get dressed, make coffee, and prep two trays of bread!

The boys wander out of their bunk beds, and the coffee is ready. The bread gets kneaded and goes in salty and seedy. Emma cooks an egg, and we all devour loaves of bread. Legos from six years living aboard are spread on the table for playing. Littles game. No school today! Kids open some presents. We motor on. I am thankful for no big wind and waves with seasick kids on this holiday at sea.

I go over the schoolwork that the teens have done this week from days past. Emma prints something and stitches something. Hmm? Nick and Tristan sail. I spend the rest of the day cross stitching and reading my guidebook in the cockpit. It's nice to have a day off.

Kids finish decorating cookies for Santa. Emma does a good decapitated one. I must get on the traditional Hirt Christmas

Eve soup, which is always filled with seafood. With hours of prep, it pulls together okay, but with mostly canned seafood. Tristan said he'd help chop, but he gets too busy sailing with his dad. Soup devoured with more warm bread, some ramen too. Clean up. Tuck in.

As is tradition, Nick reads the *Polar Express* to all the kids in the aft. Then all go their separate ways for night watches or sleeping. Littles and I watch a bit of a movie with snow, then we all shut our eyes to wait for Santa. Nick and T are on their night-shifts and the lookout.

Hero

—you've saved me.

time.
squall.
depth.

sound of voice.
touch of hand.
look of calm.

i survived.
in your lifejacket arms.

Blank Page

like no wind
like no waves
like no stars
like a fog-filled air
without a moon
on a vast, endless
motionless ocean
words appear

Sunday

Day eight. CHRISTMAS DAY! Still at sea between Tonga and New Zealand deep in the Pacific Ocean. I'm up before 4 am for my shift. Santa comes and drops off surprise presents. I try to kiss him, but he's too fast. Tristan passes the baton with his usual long speech about what I'm to do. I write a poem, "Nocturnal Sea Santa," text family, and sit to continuously monitor the wind and watch Santa's sleigh. It blows 10 and we sail around 6 with full sails. At 7 o'clock, it picks up to 15-17 knots and we go 8 knots. Kinda dicey but loving the speed. Lily's up first. Then Rory with wonder and awe. We watch *A Charlie Brown Christmas* for a bit together. Then Nick is up and Emma too. Mara eventually opens her eyes, and we wake up Tristan.

Autopilot on. Checking the seas periodically. Nothing in sight. Perfect conditions. Present time starts with Santa's gifts, then stockings, then the rest. It is plentiful and everyone looks happy and satisfied. Whew. We made it work! Christmas at sea. What seemed impossible is fruitful, intimate, and wonderful. Tristan gets a promised, hefty amount of money in a savings account. Lily gets promised a fiddle in New Zealand and a gorgeous Tongan fan. Emma gets dresses, Tongan clothes, and jewelry. Mara gets a poker set, Rory gets Nerf guns, robotics, and a hilarious disco Spiderman. Nick gets a promised scuba dive, and I get some good homemade things as well as presents I've picked for myself, oh and! Emma has knitted me a tea towel. Her stitching was a surprise for me! And very loved. Cereal and leftover bread is warmed up. We eat. I build some robotics with Rory and play some poker with Mara, and then I go for a much-needed nap. Rory comes to cuddle and game. Nick updates me on weather. We are sailing and motoring on and off to keep up speed. It's cloudy, cool, and rainy.

Lunch is leftover seafood soup or ramen, which kinda makes me feel sick, so I lay with Nick and Lily in the aft, but they keep messing with each other, while I look over more of my treasured guidebook. I go to cross stitch for a bit, then I play poker with Mara again. I do Emma's tarot cards. She is a firefly, deer, cheetah, wolf, oyster, whale, tarantula, raccoon, and shark within! We talk on making sense of it.

Then I go outside and release Ricky into the Pacific! He was my best friend from high school who passed in the previous year. "Ricky, you were a present to me, my dear friend."

I do Mara's cards. She is a spider, fish, eagle, lizard, butterfly, frog, zebra, stingray, and turtle within like her momma! She also really wanted the Zebra! Magic! We make sense of it! It's good.

I'm on dinner. The potatoes are nasty. Nick hands them to me through the galley hatch, and I toss the rotten ones into the sea. Nick plays target shooting with Rory in the cockpit, and Mara and I peel potatoes together. We eat in the cockpit: stuffed chicken, gravy, cauliflower, and party potatoes (a family recipe filled with butter and cream cheese)! Mara has a baked potato. Good Christmas dinner. Christmas dance party follows before bed with me and the littles! Epic! We get to tucking and I watch more movies with snow, before we go to bed satisfied by Santa. We made Christmas work at sea! What an accomplishment! We are two days away from New Zealand's Opua Harbor!

Nocturnal Sea Santa

whizzed by and left
wind. After two days
of motoring through
fog, rain, and clouds,
Christmas at sea
is the ability to sail.
All the lights glow red
to keep the eyes night
sharp and in honor
of him. New Zealand
is a two-day stretch away,
and my soul glows green
for a mountain spring,
a Māori carving, a nocturnal
kiwi, or a kauri forest tree.

Monday

Day nine. BELOVED BOXING DAY! That we have learned to appreciate from our time sailing the UK. But… Still at sea between Tonga and New Zealand deep in the Pacific Ocean. I'm up for my shift before 4. It is windy, but we are motoring till dawn. I write a poem, "Aim Between the Squalls." At dawn, I get Nick up to sail. He immediately goes full sail, which is too much, then dials it back. This wakes Mara and gives me an excuse to go back to bed.

I wake to Lily getting cereal. Mara asks for crepes. Nick and Emma are in the cockpit. I make crepes, and Emma and I talk on her card reading yesterday. Three of the animals have to do with hiding, and she talks on not speaking up for herself much. We talk on grandparents and war, then Lily and I talk about college and sororities. Crepes are perfectly delicious with canned peaches. Nick is off to nap. Tristan is on duty, and little Rory won't stop bouncing balls. Mara watches dog shows. Day on!

Less than hundred miles to go, we sail a sunny, close reach. Fifteen knots of wind makes us go six. School? No. It's a holiday! I work on my poetry book, let Tristan sail, and go back to reading my guidebook. I do dishes, and before long, kids are asking for food again. Nick wakes from his nap, and I'm on lasagna, ramen, cheese crisps, and shortbread with frosting. Tristan has been sailing hard and trying to make little noise, while Nick was napping, now Nick is taking over and grumpy —nothing is quite how he wants it. Must steer clear of the cockpit, so they can work it out. I go to Rory's bunkbed to get away from requests and hear lots of problems even with headphones. Mara has been seasick, and there has been fights over Lily's mermaid blanket.

When I wake, I come out to Tristan and Emma talking it up, then Tristan goes to game, and I take over sailing with Lily. She blows bubbles. Nick is a little rude, then puts himself down for another nap. We talk about family and text them. We discuss New Zealand options and watch the sea. Emma comes up after watching some shows, and I hand over the reins to cook tacos. Nick is sleeping again. He pops up in a better mood, as I put on the meat for him to dice. It is super fatty meat from Tonga. Three bowls of lard go out the window and my last packet of taco seasoning is used.

We sit in the cockpit and discuss what we need to do to enter New Zealand. It's about as complicated as the Galapagos, but we have done a lot of preparation. I go down to gather the meat, fruit, vegetables, eggs, frozen meals, because (yikes) all these items are not allowed to be brought in. Teens, Emma, and Nick gather outside to feed… dolphins! They appear for the feast of strange boat foods. They must be used to sailors doing this a day out from land. Kids sit on the side and blow more bubbles. I go down to vacuum and dice up the watermelon. Feast of watermelon and rinds over the side. Emma on clean up. I'm back with the littles.

We slow to 3 knots to get there tomorrow during light, and teens laugh with Nick in the cockpit. We have kept up the proper speed and beaten the squall from the north. It is a pleasant night of tucks due to high spirits and expectations. Early to bed. Nick and Tristan on the first two night shifts.

Aim Between the Squalls

The gale builds in the dark behind us,
and we aim between the squalls ahead.
A day's stretch from New Zealand—our
finish line of the Pacific Ocean—a year
of our lives. I cross my feet and rub
my face in the dark. I'm tired. I check
the map, adjust the course, keep up
the speed, imagine a warm bath
and bed in a home with a fire cupping
a hot drink in my hands, but here
the wind builds planning a fifty knot
gale that causes the stars to hide,
sea life to disappear, and children
to bury themselves deep in blankets.
My bones need to stretch, my legs
to run, and my sailing soul to unwind.

Tuesday

Day ten! Last day at sea between Tonga and New Zealand deep on the Pacific Ocean. I wake at 4:20 for my shift. We are going slow, and I ask Tristan to turn towards the bay, and we go in circles. This wakes Nick. We put the engine on slow to wait for sunrise. I'm on shift. Nick dumps honey and watermelon. Boys go back to bed. I write a poem, "Sweet Honey," watch the sunrise, keep an eye out, and view the countryside of New Zealand for the first time. It reminds me of the rolling hills of England.

Inside the bay, we approach a fleet of fishing boats that freaks me out. Nick comes and steers clear easily. I relax, and we take *Selkie* into Opua, New Zealand, with coffee in hand sliding between markers. Nick has a moment and cuts off the ferry to Russell. Oops. Onward. It's been a while since we've encountered other vessels. We port tie on the Q dock, get the paperwork, start to fill it out, and call customs. Everyone is on cleaning duty. Littles join in after they play with their new toys. I cancel school. A woman and man board as I'm finishing home-made bread. We are eating and clearing. They are nice. We worry about Mara, she usually says what she shouldn't, but she is goofy and funny. Then we are off to slip A11. I hit a wall with anxiety, but Nick slides *Selkie* into her dock position like honey—I'm gonna have to get some of that Manuka honey the guidebook talks about. We tie off.

Kids are anxious to explore. I take them to the internet lounge and lose my gusto. I go home to nap on an empty boat. I wake to Nick returning from checking in at the marina. Before going back to the lounge, I bring shower stuff for the kids and me. The showers are near the internet lounge and very nice. We are ten-days dirty.

When we have successfully gotten all scrubbed up and clean, we enjoy more WIFI, stop at the boat store for a kiwi courtesy flag, and then go off to the general store for a late lunch made by someone else than me! Hooray! Hummus! Wheat bread! Eggs! SIM cards! ATM! Wine! Pastries! Coffee! We snack under a tree, devour hummus on *Selkie*, and then the kids are back to the lounge. Nick works on my SIM card connection, and I journal. Emma heads to check on kids, then us too. It is the captain's turn to scrub up.

I work online and check on my graduate homework from UHI. While at sea, I have received a great grade on my final project, which was a poetic response to *His Bloody Project* by Graeme Macrae Burnet worked on with professor and writer, Mandy Haggith. Emma takes kids to playground to swing about. Lily heads back to boat—daydreaming on a boy who works here at the marina and graciously opened a door for her. Kids return. Emma plays cards with Mara. Tristan and Rory play on devices.

I search AirBnb and plan a trip around North Island designed via my precious guidebook, and then work on my world of academia. We decide on some fish and chips takeaway. Emma and I go to get it, and Rory, and Mara, and Lily, and Tristan follow when we take too long. We all find any excuse for walkabouts. We sit and wait and videos from family and friends start pouring in from State-side! I watch them at the restaurant, and we all laugh about how incredibly different our lives are.

The sun sets behind land, not sea, and we devour Ben and Jerry's ice cream. Settle back into our own beds and get a long-needed, full night's rest.

Wednesday. Slip A11, Bay of Islands Marina, Opua, North Island, New Zealand. Nick and I relax and stay in bed for as long as we can. It's been a long time apart. I make coffee and English muffins with sloppy eggs. Lily goes to get fresh fruit with the littles. Tristan puts together the guppy (our inflatable, mini catamaran). We hang about and talk about the move to our semi-permanent slip at the marina, and how I will wash all of our laundry. Emma wanders off for the whole day on a walk.

I do math and phonics with kids online, which is good, then we dress, meet the neighbor Brad, who says we are "proper explorers" in a very thick New Zealand accent. Then they take off, and we do too. We get stuck sideways in current and wind in-between the slips. Nick manages a back and forth to get us out. We head from A11 to i18 and pull in too late getting stuck sideways again. We pester off and roundabout to try again, and a catamaran is pulling out. We hold too long and really do a job on the fenders coming in, but our new neighbors are nice, and we tie the lines on both sides for a longer stay.

Kids are impatient for the lounge, so they head out with Lily. Nick goes about trying to get projects done. Tristan sticks boat side working on homework all the time asking where is Emma? I do laundry and school with the kids in the lounge. We go back and forth switching it and getting goodies at the cafe. I meet the owner, and he is astounded I drink whiskey straight. I get a bagel for Mara and a smoothie for Lily. T comes for the laundry. Only 20 bucks with one wash of four loads, and two spins in the dryer.

I finish school with the littles, journal, download boat and hiking apps, and send out Lily to look for blankets or sleeping bags. She finds nothing. It is summer here, but we are used to the equator's heat. I look for Airbnb stays for our grandparents' visit in February.

Back at the boat, Nick has fixed the back toilet seat, and I fold the laundry. Emma returns with a local job at a kayak rental place, and we head off to dinner at the yacht club. It is like a buffet type, order yourself, clean yourself deal. Teens go to get sweatshirts. It's a bit chilly outside, then our restaurant buzzer goes off, and we get nuggets, fries, salmon, veggie burgers, and a lamb salad. The food is so good here, and it is so fun to take care of the waitress stuff ourselves. We already are in love with the laidback culture we feel.

The birds swarm and we throw leftovers into the sea that they fight over. It is nice to watch other boats having problems after our morning of switching births—that was hard. New Zealand currents are strong! Note taken! Emma discusses her day of hitchhiking and job searching. Kids walk the pier. Nick cleans up, and we do too. I catch Rory peeing off the pier, locals are fishing, and we enjoy the sunset. Then back to *Selkie*, tucks, shows, bedtime. New Zealand is underfoot, and the adventure of seven months is only just underway.

Sweet Honey

In the darkness, navigating
by instruments, we slip into
the Bay of Islands like sweet
honey eases down the side
of the jar, falls midair, coats,
envelopes ingredients, warms
the soul, or sticks to fingers.
New Zealand's rigid complexity
shadows itself in a muddy orange
sunrise. Stars remain freckled
in the sky like her flag. A lighthouse
spins off a cliff into the sea, and I
am like a bee all abuzz with my
new destination, new nectar.

PART II

Kauri Tree World Osmosis

An Important Note:

To the Māori and complex tangata whenua, people of the land, in New Zealand, the people of Te Ika-ā-Māui, the Fish of Maui, North Island, and Te Wai Pounamu, the Waters of Greenstone, South Island.

I am a sailing traveler that admired your home greatly, trying my best to absorb your myths, legends, words, and traditions into my own. At no point, do I mean to offend if what I use, I have used incorrectly. It was an honor to walk the grounds you have inhabited.

Thank you for sharing your part of the earth with my family.

Aquatic
Sail Into Roots

Opua

The fog settles.
Selkie sleeps,
and I cannot.

The hull tingles
with the ocean
like goosebumps

on the skin—New
Zealand, our new
home. My body

is tied to the dock
like lines cleat
her arms and legs.

My mind says explore,
but I can't move.
First, I must adjust

to land and let wind
pass on by — feel
the water through

rain. Roots lengthen.

Selkie gets hauled out,
and my aqua eyes
turn pounamu green.

Bay of Islands

Tossed off the dock.   Insufficient.   Like a fish, I get rowdy.

I slip, flap, reflect — .   Moonlight in bird squawk.

I snake, pig, eel — starved.   No food left

in the ocean.   The boy watching says, he wants

a turn to be shark, to be bird.   Like fingers of ocean,

I wiggle, slip, flap like octopus tentacles.   I devour.

The dark moves.   Killer black in my soul.

Reflection in the water shows my life — blue,

yellow, black.   I am the reflection, the universe of things,

unknown — figures in kraken hair,
a key to the movement of stars.

Great Barrier Island

Passing you filled with wētapunga,
I try to breathe in, creep along, slowly
sail. Stars drop through me anchoring
heavily inside my rib cage like stories,
stories that create in capillaries, smell
of endangered species, lighthouse hums,
cape cliff corners, caves, night stillness,
sea-level tide stains, ticklish branches
caressed with insect grip. You're shaped
like a seal just escaped Auckland, city life,
sky towers, graffiti, cement, to sanctuary
of the sea enveloped in cyclones, Pacific
troubles. Be there but be unattainable
like a ship sunken in the sea, a shark smell
of human, a fish outside the net, a lobster
that scuttles beside the trap, a salsa
dance with no partner. Be you. Island
Great. Barrier to land dwellers. Mystery
to sailors setting course to evade you.

Patience– Something you have when you have the time

Well. We were out of time.

The Bay of Plenty, the waters east of Auckland and north of the huge peninsula that juts out east containing Gisborne and the Raukumara Range, took control of our sailing vessel, *Selkie*. My husband and I, with our four children, white-knuckled the helm and psychologically threw up our hands up. Winds blew so powerfully from behind us that there was no turning, especially no turning around. We were headed to Cape Runaway, and the ocean had run away with our boat. The feeling was not helplessness. It was like riding a train with no breaks. Just go with it. Hope for the best.

The Bay of Plenty had become an ice cream scoop for the Pacific, turning out some nasty wind and waves. We were in a toy boat, and the Pacific Ocean was playing with us. Our ice cream was becoming a sloshy mess—goopy in the bowl. The main was reefed, head sail in, stay sail out, and all the kids but my eldest were seasick. The waves beat us on the side, scooping up from land, and pushed us hard from aft. My current technique was feeding the crew lots of bread—baguettes, grilled cheese, quesadilla… Whatever they could keep down to settle them.

Onwards to make the turn south felt impossible. We attempted to edge starboard, but it seemed it would break *Selkie*, even though she weighs over twenty-two tons. This sail was a one-way ticket on a Japanese MLX01 Maglev that was bound to not make it up and down the mountains. It was not smooth. It was violent, right before there was enough sea room to turn south, then… nothing. Absolutely nothing. We had escaped and slipped out of the scoop. No wind. Sails in. Motor on.

Power to Napier. Crew spirits soar! Admiration of ocean slowly returned.

And this is where we were for weeks. This is where I should have had more patience.

Napier is an amazing, rebuilt, art deco town that has recovered after a horrible earthquake in 1931, and there is so much to see and do.

The sailing club we docked at contained the nicest people we had yet met in New Zealand. We experienced all we could via bus, and New Zealand kids would take out their Opti's, small learning sailboats, past our boat on the weekends and after school on the weekdays. We would root for them from our hatches. Super brave kids teaching themselves to sail in this location leaves no questions as to how they will be as adult sailors. We truly could have stayed here for a very long time, but our buddy boat was waiting for us in Wellington, our Scottish friends on *Lucky Girl*, and we were anxious and too excited to get to them.

I picked the weather window convinced that the mainland would protect us from the winds like it did when we turned the corner after Cape Runaway. This was a very bad theory.

We slipped out of our cozy home in Napier, where we were spoiled, and headed into the open South Pacific Ocean again. This stretch must be timed perfectly. When you reach Cook Strait, there is no getting into Wellington, if the Tasman Sea is blowing west to east. Tacking leaves you going back and forth in one spot and motoring barely gets you a knot, even if full throttle.

My calculations aimed us for a 5 am wind change that would shoot us into Wellington.

Again, patience would be required. The whole trip would take three days.

Right around Cape Turnagain, day two, the winds began in the night.

"Reef it, T!" shouted my husband, Nick, to our eldest, Tristan.

I clung to my youngest two in the aft cabin in the dark, and I could hear my teenage daughter move from the v-birth to the couch for more stability.

Bang! The waves were like hitting brick walls, so loud. We were taking 40 knots on the beam, and I was regretting my decisions and my lack of patience.

My third child, Mara, stayed in bed by planting her feet against my side table, whereas my youngest and I were sliding off the sheets to the floor, so I wrapped him in my arms, braced my feet against the bed, and slept in my husband's chair, port and high side of *Selkie*.

Bang! *Floosh!* Water poured in through the crack of the top hatch and streamed across our bed and bodies.

I lock down the hatches.

Great. I thought. *Now I must get mass amounts of towels involved.*

Bang! Through the night and the next day. My role? Damage control.

Then it was gone, and we had timed the Cook Strait correctly. 5 am.

But the wind did not do what it said it would on all our prediction tools.

Noon.

3 pm.

Nope.

We tack back and forth out in the South Pacific staring at Cape Palliser and Palliser Bay.

Please let us in, I begged.

Nope.

We tried motoring.

No chance.

"I vote we forget Wellington and head for the Marlborough Sounds," my husband suggested, and my stubborn mind said, *No! I am gonna see Wellington, and this ridiculous wind and water from the Tasman is gonna do what it promised!*

5 pm.

The waves started sitting and swirling.

Twelve hours off from prediction?

I'll take it!

Full sail! Full motor! The sun began to set in the brightest of hues, and our patience, or lack of, was rewarded with the current from the South Pacific push, and the Tasman backing off.

In the dark, in Oriental Bay, southwest anchorage below Wellington, this *bang, clang* of the windlass equipment was so comforting, as the anchor *splashed* down into the depth of fifty feet and held strong into the murky, bottom mud.

We all slept hard.

Knock. Knock. On the hull. *Grrr. Ruff, ruff.*

We were awoken by *Lucky Girl* and their new dog, Hamish, that came to see us via dinghy, because they held no patience for us to take our slip at their maria later that day.

We had survived another crossing, and now we had time.

Cape Runaway

Never look back, or don't
take your eyes away. The sea
has control of you now.

One way ticket round East Cape. Surfing up
like a dolphin plays in a wave, water takes you,
drops you, slams you, up, over, down, between.

Aim for the inside of the bank, outside
the riptide for a South Pacific turn
that will give waves a chance to flip you.

Vulnerable, you are destination, vulnerable,
you are destruction, you are conditions unknown.

Waves break behind
and starboard. Life jackets
tethered, body swaying, up and over,
guardians of moving, sailing, changing.

Sailors. Surrounded by condition.

Knowing
the swallowing
sea, knowing
those looming mountains
carry no bay, no sanctuary,
and tumble on like the crest of the wave.

Somehow. Somewhere.

There will be an end.

A Nightshift

Silence under the stars—
Thrumming motor pushing, praying,
Obeying the rush to Napier.
Right from the bow, from the south,
More winds than predictable will rise.

Calm the sea sits, waiting to realize—
Overcome the surface with gust, gale.
Moon hides, scared of the outcome.
Eventually wind wins, the invisible
Strength that decides on sailors.

From Cape Turnagain

to Cook Strait

We should have turned around. Instead
we cuddled in blankets as the room

spilled geography, medicine, mathematics.
The bed shed us like skin. We clung

but slipped free to floor again and again.
Discarded, used, and unneeded by boat.

The weather window was broken
from the start. It blew open across land

making fun of us for imagining. The galley
threw her coffee pots, turned space into noise,

made us regret, hold, fumble, fall, grasp
at the night. The hatches shared

the ocean dropping streams across beds
to make us sea serpents in dreams we

fought to have. My smallest daughter
whispers, *it's worth it*, and the world

is attainable with her bravery. Her hand
in mine in a capsule in the South Sea.

Underground
Anchored Roots

Waitomo Caves

ThisPlace keeps me up at night,
perhaps not the breeze off the shore that ticklesTrees,
or the birds that discussWeather,
but the room that traps me in tunnelsUnderwater
—slimy, blueBlack. It puts the taste of thick greenMoss
in my mouth and loudCrickets in my head.
I tremble there in the dark, starless with stars that aren'tStars,
with carnivorousCannibalistic glow
worms' strings —spittingShittingSlithering down
the room'sWalls. Why can a sibling
eating larvae keep me looking? How do I somehowFind
comfortInTheEarth
with them? They steal myEyes
from the runningWater and the sixty-five metersOfStone.
ifloat.
HandsUp. InchingAlong.
Trying not to disturb these evil, mushroomInsect maggots
thatTake as long asHuman
babies toDevelop.
ToLive only four days. FourDays
toMate and lay over a hundredEggs and die
of exhaustion. The waterMoves for days.
Pulling meAlong neverending.

The darknessFlows. I try toDrift, continue, slipSlither unnoticed.

Wistful on Waianga

Be cause Bec ause Beca use
My mind won't let me sleep—
The wind snores through the window—
The rain speaks to me in Morse code—
The earth grows up through the bed posts—
Roots lift me above the mattress, instead—

Instead of digging me deeper, the living mole—
Blind—Is pulled out of my depths with claws—
That scratch gently wondering on me—
The warmth it once had is gone—

I turn over in my bed trying to sleep—
Another way, and the water in the air—
Calls my name—Mag da lena, Magdalena—
Magda lena louise, and I am awake—

Finding more creatures within me—

Trout of Tūrangi

To munch on a manuka
beetle,
& gobble a grass-grub
nettle, the hunger
growls within me. Three
currents form
to slither
& descend
to challenge me
upstream,
my muscular length
like a spring flips
& flops my pink sides up
the ladder
to breed. Netted
traps must be avoided
& predator jaws
must be
averted. Inaki
& Kupenga,
by canoe, by net, will search
for me, interrupt
my breeding.
I will flish
& flip to set loose, airborne,
& upstream. Wading
men, green-booted, capture
& kill my young,
a generation.
They've thrived: Fishermen
& the hungry. Stealing
& harvesting my plump
young. For now, I must feed

watching
the riverbed
for grubs,
watching
the rivertop
for flies,
a crispy cricket,
& a crunchy centipede.
Time
only a disturbance
of water.

Mt Cook

Like mixing a stew, bunnies
spin in thousands at the base
of the mountains. Poison signs
warn dog owners and young
children of the risks. Native
species, flightless birds, plants,
are the priority, and the thoughtless
bunny eats a snack, brings succulent
sweets back to the den, and delivers
death to brothers and sisters, mothers
and fathers. Mt Cook looms, cold
and distant, beautiful and dangerous.
Hikers, locals, tourists spill through
the valley. Selfie here, oblivious there,
snapping. I watch, contemplating
population, avalanches, footprints, the softness
of fur, the miscommunication of a photograph.

Pause on Lake Tekapo

The water intake, lake-side machine,
has me up at night. Made for environmental
disaster—earthquake, flood—
it sits, unused by the water. Hurricane
Bret tips through the Caribbean
on the other side of the world, storms
and earthquakes, occur every other day
in New Zealand, and I am swept up, churned
inside the intake machine, part of the water
that is considered troublesome. Fire churns
below, and sunshine burns above. I'm twisted
into the depths to distinguish, but I
transform to steam—full of hot air—
a bodiless form with open eyes.

Forest Floor

Uncurling Fern

Stella. My sheep dog. Nips at the heels of the herd mountainside. She gets them to stop and huddle together with a stare. She's gathered the full forty-three for me this morning. The sun rises turning the empty village across the bay orange in its quiet stillness.

Fweet, my high-pitched, airy whistle carries to her in the empty air, and she answers quickly by running to my side. I reward her with a scratch around the ears. She's got more matted dreads again. My long dark blond hair has developed some too.

Stella's one blue eye and one green sympathizes with my blueberry color, and she follows me willingly down to the brambles for lunch. The oysters I found at low tide this morning didn't satisfy me like they should have. The ocean tastes different. I plucked them open to find microplastics like confetti. Instead of sliding it into my mouth, I had to rinse them. It didn't feel like it was doing much good. They tasted infused with the flavor of factory. But the blackberries are plump and plenty in the summer heat. No one else to pick them. They burst in my mouth and crunch in my teeth, so I roll over in my mind again my recipe for jam as to not forget. *Three handfuls of blackberries, one peach, honey, a bit of crushed seeds, with a squeeze and zest of lemon. Good thing this patch of land was riddled with orchards before the end. Trees and brambles, ocean and mountain stream are all I need.*

Huff, whine, ip, ip, Stella reminds me she's hungry. I'll have to catch a fish for her later, but I don't have much patience, so I hope that one of my traps has caught something small. She can hunt a little on her own, but I don't like her to wander too far from me.

"I do wish you were a vegetarian, girl." I pat her on the head. "Berries are so good, and there are plenty. At least you like bananas." She responds to my cheerful voice with a wag of her bushy matted tail. It's been a long time, since I ate any human race remnants from my childhood, like my favorites: baked beans, sliced pineapples, dark chocolate. It's been seven years since I lost my family and most of the world in a pandemic. Now it's me. Me and Stella.

Grrr! Arrr! Yip! The stray dogs fight in the distance. Stella and I watch in silence. Glad they are keeping to themselves.

The smell of burning bark reaches our noses, and we turn our heads to the east up the bay. What the sunrise had shielded with morning fog and dew reveals a fire in the distance. Not wide and moving like a wild cleansing one, but a singular stream, rising like an upside-down waterfall. *Human.*

We turn our back to it. We know what to do all too well. *Hide.* Back to our cave entrance off the river, where during the day all the long-legged, lengthy cave crickets, wēta crickets, join us to hide from the birds, and glow worms keep us company—a starry night sky in the day.

Stella and I move along the brambles and tree line. We can't cut across the field where the *human* might notice our movement. We'll have to move the herd the rest of the way in the night towards the other side of the mountain. "Lily. Hide and seek," my mother's voice comes to me. "Take care of Stella. She'll keep you company."

I throw a stick for Stella to keep her along the tree line as well. I feel my mother's touch on my cheek, pick a wildflower to put seaside in her memory, and wish to myself to have let her hug me more often. *I could use a hug.*

Bang! A shot rings out. *This human has a gun.* Stella and I speed up our pace and duck further into the trees.

The cave entrance is close. I gather my clothes set out to dry and all traces that I live there. Stella licks up some fresh water, and I scoop some into my mouth. Fresh. Cold. Replenishing.

"Stella, baby. You're gonna have to eat some crickets again for dinner tonight." And the day is done, before it barely started, but if I want another one—this is what we must do.

Stella scurries into the sharp-edged rock crevice, and her matted fur disappears. I look one more time at the blue sky and blazing afternoon sun. *I'm alive, Momma. I'm still here.* And the darkness envelops me like her womb. The whole world needs a re-birthing, a new beginning, a vengeance of life. It fought back. Now it sleeps. *I'll sleep with you.* Stella curls up next to me with a sigh. A cricket moves its antennae smelling the change of heat I bring to the air. And the water moves on and through past my makeshift nest. *The world was a delicate egg, and we cracked it. It ate itself. Ate its outer layer with a virus. Cleaning her surface.*

"Tonight, Stella. Under the stars, we'll live." And both our heavy eyelids drop down like blankets.

When in Russell

When the breeze blows up past the tree ferns
When the sun sets lavender and kiwis wander the grass
When a husband naps and shakes happily in deep sleep
When the smallest children enjoy four bubble baths a day
When the hike to the beach involves a moss-covered cliff
When the shells sit on the beach like a blanket
When the freezer welcomes endless ice cream
When the flowers and birds won't stop their gossiping
When the clouds float in the sky just for me off the porch
When a microwave gives steaming snacks in twenty seconds
When the walls and floor don't move with the strength of wind
When the beams of the roof have no hatches to shut
When the earth dirt gets stuck to my exploring legs
I know I am on deep, strong, comforting land
But the boats in the bay bob — whispers that beg

Fern Blood—Manipulated

Opua, Paihia, Karikari, Reinga, Waipapakauri, Kaitaia, Wairere, Ōmāpere—
The names get tangled on my tongue like a road that won't stop turning,
A ditch that gravitationally pulls me off the designated path. I spin the words
Into a hike that doesn't have makeshift stairs, guardrails, bridges, or info labels.
A darkness in the crevice of a rock calls to me, though I won't stay—no sheets.

On land, I haven't picked out what color sand is my flavor, there's a need to now.
A man walks too close to the road we ride, and a strange rift tears inside me for him.
Turn, turn, pull, turn, ride curves of countryside like millions of years grew thinking.
The water shapes my curves giving my skin ripples, wrinkles, spots, crevices, charm.
I am rattled from this land, and my eyes can't look away as a cut sprouts fern blood.

Harman Hike Howl

Things like this led to that. Pouring, drenching, thundering rain in the Southern Alps with husband and son on the Harman Pass at 1 am taking shelter in cliffside in over 55 mph winds atop the summit. Things like this led to that.

"Just decide," I said. The new Garmin Inreach tracker was set, not to perfect communications due to lack of WIFI on the side of the mountains that followed the river in the middle-of-nowhere New Zealand, but trackable for his begged-for, two-night, three-day hike over Harman Pass to Arthur's Pass.

"It just doesn't feel right," he said. He, being my 16-year-old son. Spikes for his shoes for possible snow encounters were purchased in Greymouth. A day of rest with pre-packing at a beach-side campground, and *hmm, I don't know if it will ever feel right?!*

"How about dropping me off on the other side?" he asked.

"What?! That is not researched or planned or possible with the RV," I ranted annoyed. I had so much work to do for my dissertation on my second masters, teaching my other three kids, and wanting to explore myself. *Argh, how to satisfy a teenager.*

Yes. These things led to that. At Jacksons Retreat, I convinced the gentle woman with a child and a small puppy to take my husband and sixteen-year-old son to the drop off point and leave.

I stare at my seven-year-old son sleeping with me while his father is gone, as the rain pounds down so hard it shakes the campervan to tipping point. I check the tracker, then check it again. Only a gentle rain and some small winds were predicted. *Trusting that was a mistake.* My independent, risk-taking boys had decided to hike up the mountain in the dark before the heavy rains turned the track into a river but stopped around 1 am. It was 2:30 am. *Mudslide? Broken leg? Frozen? Starving? Did I encourage this? Is it making them happy?* 3:30. 4:30. I have an online class for my dissertation at 5 am due to time change from UK to NZ, and though terrified for members of my family, I decide to go through with it. *Can't sleep. Don't want to reschedule.* Meeting occurs. Sleeping kids don't mind. *Just something to add to the torrential rain downpour that feels like we are sinking in the ocean.* 5:30. 6:30. No word.

My message: I'm contacting Mountain Rescue at 9 am, if I don't hear from you. Sending an email to Department of Conservation now to alert them of your whereabouts.

Ting. "I'm contacting Mountain Rescue at 9 am, if I don't hear from you. Sending an email to Department of Conservation now to alert them of your whereabouts."

"Shit." The tent wind pressure pushed it at an angle into his face. The condensation dripped. *Hypothermia. I can feel it.*

"T. T! Tristan. We gotta move. Your mom is worried. We gotta push on.

Was that five hours of sleep? If I hold my hands together, will they stop trembling? Will my whole body stop trembling? Boots. Move.

Ting. 7:30. "We are on the trail moving, and everything is okay."

How?! Thank the gods. Why do I encourage these things.

Yep. Things like this led to that. Pouring, drenching, thundering rain in the Southern Alps with husband and son on the Harman Pass hiking in the dark wind and rain on the summit. Things like this led to that.

Raglan

The cicadas vibrate, and the night
pulls me into unusual pancake rocks.
Mount Karioi grabs the clouds, holds
them above Pirongia Forest, and a bee
stings my shoulder in the dark. Horea
ghosts beneath the bush pulsate me
into a winter blizzard during summer.
The North Island keeps me awake.
Dreams fall from my mouth to swirl
into a landing tattooed onto my chin.
The fern opens permanently, moko
kauae, and I must lead my ancestors
through my life, spirits worn as a feather
robe. Lips black, mind rooted, soul
on journey through the depths of caves.

Papa-tū-ā-nuku
Earth Mother

Like me from the burrow, heavy with egg,
my mate and I scurry into Tangotango,
blackness of night. My bristly hair, earth
color, protects me in the shadows. I hear
him claw, sniff, eat mostly nut and seed.
He will protect my egg, my ngahuru pōtiki,
my autumn birth, our fifth nest together.
Leaf crunch, log rot, tree bark, worm hunt,
beetle scurry, ant eat, grub squirm,
squished berry, plump fungi feast. Night,
Rangi-nui, sky father, you have fulfilled your
Papa-tū-ā-nuku, earth mother, with delicious
sweets. No stoats or cats squeak or hiss,
hurry at us in the night. Tāne-mahuta,
god of forests and birds, protects us.
Our nest is ready. It rains. Rangi-nui cries
onto Papa-tū-ā-nuku. Another good sign. Tears
that plump the berry, soften the seed.

The Sky Opened

And let a river
Fall upon us.
Like the weight
Of the ocean,
Water pushed
Down from
Mountainside
Turning us in
Legend like
Quiet bystanders
Reading a tragedy.
Sleepless, only later
Pondering the separation
Of reality and dream.
How can the air
Hold so much water?
It's the sound of anger.
We are blamed—
Judged by the earth
For watching.

Understory
The Wind Talks

Māniania Kōtiro: Noisy Girl

It's silent again. My enemy is silence because I never like silence inside my head. Music plays, birds talk to me, grass sings to me. The world buzzes, and I feel it in every part of me from my ankles to my neck—my head and feet blossoming with it, but then at times, I lose my hearing and my thoughts stop. It terrifies me. I need movement, music, crickets, waves, cooking noise in the kitchen of our kāuta, cooking house. When things go silent. I panic. Maybe that is why they named me, Mara. I came out screaming in waves like the ocean, my mother said, and Mara means the sea. I am the daughter of a wai mākutu, water magic, a wisher of fine weather, and I will be a wai mākutu as well.

My father was frightened of me, but he always preferred my quiet sister who does everything he says when he says it. She's bound to be an ao mākutu, like him, made from the mountains and hills, filled with earth magic. I don't like to listen to him. He tells me to do something, and I go to the sea that crashes close to the sheep, the horses, the chickens, and the pigs. I scrub the grum from the farm off my feet, right before I run through the animals and get it right back between my toes again.

They say I was born with dark black hair like my grandmother Meri. She was a maruāpō makutu, made of the stars with magic of the moon. That's another reason for my name—a version of hers. But then my hair turned red like my father's (he really held me a lot those days), until finally light, sandy brown like my mother's. They say my spirit is like hers. Sometimes when I run to the seashore, she is already there doing the same. Both of our enemies are silence, so we sing to the water together to weave words into the waves—make spells. We are always synchronized, in tune, in harmony, with fire and spirit of the untamed shore.

Recently the humidity of the ocean has curled my long hair, and it drives my sister crazy. She always wanted curly hair. At least that's one thing I have that she wants. She never wants my company. I'm too dramatic and emotional, she says, just like a storm on the sea. She's another reason I run to the water. I will sail away from here someday. Travel and sing. Travel and sing. Cast spells to better the earth and strengthen the ocean. Travel and sing. And other whānau, tribes, will come to hear me. They will ask for me by name. Where is Mara the Musical? Musical Mara, the wai mākutu, with the curls of the ocean in her sandy hair? Will she sing to us? Will she cross the sea? I turn ten next month, before I'm twelve, they will call for me from Whakatū to Waiharakeke, from Ōtautahi to Ōtepoti, from Rakiura to Tāhuna. For I don't care about the North Island, Te Ika-a-Māui. Only the strong, South Island, Te Wai Pounamu matters to me. South Island and sea. Conjuring with water.

My love is out there in a noisy place. I can feel him. He is of the water too. His spirit calls to me when it rains. My thatch that hangs over my window in the rectangular house flaps in the wind, bangs on the timber, and the rain trickles in. I know he will be an impatient boy, so I run to him, and let the noise of the rain envelope my whole being.

I must have been of the Marakihau, sea monsters, in my last life, half sea, half human, able to transform in the salty sea, swallow sailors. My mother too. The both of us always wearing our sea skin, playing in the noise of the whale killers, swimming circles around the boats that poach sea life.

My mother recently had a boy, my baby brother, Tāwhiri. He will be of fire. She's very busy with him, and my sister with my father, and my oldest brother with his spears, stones, and poi. He is an ea makutu, manipulating and capturing air with weapons and instruments. I prefer to sing with just my voice and nothing else. There needs to be attention purely on only the melody, my melody, so I am here on the shore making noise.

On the beach, with my wet feet, I especially like to speak to the brothers of the four winds that I stand through. Wind and water, Tā and wai, have always been close. Talking with both helps with my spell casting. They talk to me and tell me their names. *Tūāraki, north wind*, who warms me, or *Tonga,* when the rain comes up from the south, chilly and cold. Marangai, my friend from the east that showers me with love, or Hauāuru, from the west, the one that tickles with otherworld dust. When the sky looks like stretched feathers and the wind blows sideways, I whisper *aowhēkere*, because it howls at me, and I must tempt it to settle. But *aopakarea* is my favorite. It's a thunderstorm cloud that shouts and breaks from the sky, and then an āniwaniwa appears, the color curve, the rainbow. Mom says, that's my color, every color.

So, now, it's silent again—the middle of the night when my enemy finds me. When there is nothing, when there is no noise, when not even the wind comes to me off the Tangaroa, the sea. I must imagine myself underwater with nothing singing, only my eyes making music with the visions of phosphorescent jellies. My wai mākutu soul settles. Then and only then, I tolerate the silence.

Listen to Te Wahapu Inlet

The year spreads before me
like the ocean rests
like the ocean challenges
The enchantment floats up thickening the air
How do we not see
How do we not sea
We must prepare for our journey
of endless blue water
of bottomless depths
The sun shines mountainside orange, and…
the Māori turtle, te honu,
the seal, te rāpoka,
the whale, te tohorā
the kiwi, and the takahe rest
We prepare like the kea, the wēta punga, the tuatara

And words form like an albatross over water, te toroa,
a brave pīwakawaka at the edge of the forest
Letters spin like a shark, te mangō taniwha, a stoat, te toriura
Feel and speak, communicate and fulfill our plans
like a kākāpō speaks to snow within a
mountain fiord
like a pāngurunguru whispers to the distance, to the next shore
Place it inside the tongue

My legs grow
My fingers move down the bark of the tree
My mind stays under the giant fern
watching the sun trickle
through the leaves to my skin

Here, this, now will be the egg—plump, productive, purposeful

There are spells
in the water, in the hills,
in the movement of the breeze

Let the telling grow in silence,
Size and shape, until the ship emerges

from the lips
and carries
unknowns
to strangers' eyes that swim like letters to an anchor

Haruru

Hills move like ocean waves here,
and I buzz like an insect with energy.

Sheep rest near fences pressing their borders.
They look to me for something to chew on,

as their mouths grind side to side, I see,
and a burgundy flower inside me grows.

The wind makes the gate tremble and creak,
and trees bend forever sideways, trying

to detach the roots and pull up from the earth.
Letters drop into place, unscrambled,

I breathe, and the hill in the distance dimples.
The rain comes when the night is asleep,

and a story in the drops dance with no music
making me a writer waiting, rusty, hot, bubbling.

Ink rests deep in skin,
and the Waitangi Treaty is signed. Kauri
tree cries and creaks, grows and looks
down. Foot and tongue stomp earth. Fern
explodes. Shadows exploited. Boundaries
drawn that were stamped with wax white
seals, superior firepower. Sperm whale
bone, hoeroa, set down for feather quill.
Queen Victoria aiming to settle a world—
a world away—soft percussion of poi balls,
strong thrust of taiaha, tongue of defiance.

Strapped. Tied. Cut Open. Waiting.

Back on our boat again. She survived Cyclone Gabrielle, and the extra lines that were used to hold her in place speak to me that she has been captured. She must be set free. First, we open her hatches, sticky from time. We roll up the bimini to let the kiwi air rush through her, cleansing. We untie all the knots holding her dinghy on the bow and use the halyard to lift her up, open another hatch, and now we have full breath sliding through to renew her from our absence. Boats need people. They rot away without constant care. *Selkie* needs her head scrubbed. Her galley burning. Her motor humming. Her sails dusted in bay wind, ocean spray, pull of hull, and us. She needs us.

FinGers FiGure

I write best when all the world crumbles around me
and all there is, is stars and ocean. In the middle
of nowhere like a spaceship drifting through another

world with weeks upon days upon weeks of nothing.

I write best when I can't get off my boat. There is no-
where to walk or go but my cockpit and galley, my
cockpit and galley. This is where I find me in my head.

Voices of the world can't reach me, and I just wonder

on them. I wonder on doings of land, those that use
their legs, but I use my fingers. On my phone, on my
computer, I let my fingers figure my thoughts into

a white space in the black space of night and the letters

that type on the page slip through like cracks on the white
screen to the rest of the world. They dwindle there, not
to be seen for months, then with the magic of night

and air, they crack into land dwelling lives when time

has been set aside to relate out there, nowhere, in here.

Gale in Hawke's Bay

I don't know why the wind talks
to me and tells me to move, whistles at me
and tells me
to dance, yells at me and tells me
to show my face? It might be because
the water has pulled me
under and told me to see through
the surface, told me to hold my breath
as I use all my arms
and legs to reach another level, told me
to taste the saltiness of the earth,
or perhaps, it's because
the fireside already took my eyes past
the darkness, took my eyes into deep
orange contemplation,
took my eyes into memory. Yet… don't
put it past the earth, which holds me
tight and wrestles me
back against the whistling, clanging,
fighting, punching, slamming secret.

Blossoming

through the branches, the moon
creates tendrilled crags of branches
that steal my breath in beauty. Why
does the thick forest of the mountainside
know my name? Fog settles like a necklace.
Wear me, it whispers, and the girl
with the messy, matted hair stares
at me in the dark, sleepless. Down
the roots grab and hold my eyes
that search for treetops. The wind
slowly slithers along my jaw and spine
to conjure words for the darkness
that holds me in a sublime, surreal
cocoon. Only the owl and kiwi see me
tonight encircled in need to write.

Canopy

Floating Leaf Letter

Me—Turning Wētā Punga

Wētā—meta—kafka—morphosis
urge skin to exoskeleton—actuality
no more extra layers around middle
or thigh—my six spiny legs with slim
appeal, my antennae stretching smelling
evergreen Karaka—poisonous seed
tempting male wētā punga—we are not
"Gods of Ugly Things"—my ovipositor
makes eggs and moon mine—antennae
whisk air around me into aura—to quake
Monarch—inspire ether dance—tasting
dabbing with my palps—to enjoy darkness
hook lift of my long back left leg for stretch
upright long—and tall before I bring it back
hold branch—climb higher—moonset
cloud cover dims—whale spout bursts
the ocean—the male black swan croons,
bugle-like, croons in nest—a Tūī lands
smaller than me—frightened by my size
takes flight from Te Hauturu-o-Toi—
Little Barrier Island—flying—land hopping
but does not match—what I have become
here writing verse—on my unstable bark—
wet moss—silent sway—treetop—midnight tune
slow and heavy—elusive—flightless—rare

Cyclone Gabrielle

Hungry for more land, I move
south. Humans scramble for food,
water, power, light, as I dance down
the coast determined to steal illusions
of control. Kauri and kawakawa perform
the haka war dance in excitement of arrival. The rain
glistens on harakeke as humans hide, but my winds
don't terrify or tear apart. They leave them
in dark to contemplate like a kiwi
with no flight, a Moa—extinct. Hiding bones.

Writing Kumeū

When the gale in my mind blows the branches
from west to east, the "wrong way," the words
move like leaves and beg me for color, a chance
to fall. When the gale in my mind turns from north
to south, I fight through the cold-front that freezes
words in place and break them free with my hatchet.
When the gale in my mind blows from south to east,
words warm me and swirl on the page released
from coconut milk. But when the gale blows
from east to west, the way it should, I won't write.
I'll save the words for myself—tender, unused.

Hanging Haiku

{water stir} — (wind fight)
[leaf fire] … !wood crackle! … /boat heave/
cling anchor % _to poem_

air more crisp than snow
.motionless, marina tied.
// sails pause on the tongue \\

Last Frost)(ferN unfurL
Giant Wētā)(nympH emergE
Wind Rests)(haikU formeD

dance* words in sunshine*
~float letters ~endless ocean
reef the sails #poemstorm

The Ridge

Mountain mist presses into me like wind on water,
And I bend to its will comfortable within its fingers.
The tree line releases the fog, and the eel escapes
Forests of seaweed within Lake Rotoiti. Mount Robert
Embraces feathers that show me their borders. Fantail,
The pīwakawaka, shouts his domain, dangerously
Close to me, the giant human, squawking, unafraid.
Admiration, is an understatement. A fist-sized bird
Bossing me around. The Southern Alps peak around
The bend like the pīwakawaka, and I want to shout
My place as well, but I step back, and I am satisfied
To share space with elements, step lightly, calmly,
Like leaves that submit to change, turn shade, ginger.
I focus back on Lake Rotoiti, who took me to awe
The ridge of Robert, the ridge of St Arnaud, and I
Ponder names in the vast smallness of universe,
Not all the stars, but the mountain, and its sway.
Was Robert a friend that I never knew, was Arnaud
The child I never had, was their ridge my kayak
Through the thoughts that brought me here
In the woods, walking with my two daughters?

Emergent

Marama Portal

Hello, World

"Mana":
prestige, authority, control, power, influence, status, spiritual power, charisma - mana is a supernatural force in a person, place or object.
—Mt. Ruapehu's Tūroa

Crunch. Crunch. Step. Breathe. Breathe. Sigh. Sniff.

"Hello, World. This is Tristan William Hirt. I'm in Mount Ruapehu. Starts with an R. Ends with a U. The tallest mountain on the North Island of New Zealand. I started my ascent at 11 o'clock. It is now 1:14, aka 13:14. Almost at the top. 9,177 feet. Possibly a few feet off there, but I'm pretty sure that is what it was."

His phone falls from grip into the crisp, crunchy snow, and he falls to his knees among the rocks to pick it up and catch his breath. The summit is in view in the distance, and fog covers all views from the mountaintop. Rocks and lack of vegetation make it seem otherworldly. Crags of former explosions jut out from under melting snow. Rocks of black, brown, off-white speckle rims and trails that can possibly be followed. There are no other footprints but his own.

"I'm gonna put the phone down, and yeah. Yeah. Fun."

Researched mountains for years. Got good shoes. Got good instructions. Took the only day available, cloudy or not, and ascended on his own.

Wishing Dad was here. He'd make me laugh. Next time. Together.

He warned me on the sign. It read:

Volcanic Risk

Eruptions can occur at any time, with no warning!

Ruapehu is an active volcano. It has produced 145 eruptions that have impacted the upper mountain and summit plateau since 1940. The closer you are to the Crater Lake and the longer you stay, the more risk you are exposed to.

It had warning parameters. Stay out of the parameters.

The picture flashes in his mind.

Picture of crater with two outer circles. The first said, "DOC recommends you do not enter this area." It was just around the crater. The second said, "DOC recommends you do not camp or overnight in this area." DOC, yeah. Department of Conservation. Yeah. Better listen to them.

He stops for a moment near the crater lake at the summit. Lifts out his phone and spins slowly to tell the world. Too high for vegetation, rock-filled, snow pockets, peaks, a tight ridge line, fog, and more fog. The crater, filled with water that won't freeze, is close, moon-like. Magma stirs below.

He remembers the 2009 News Report of the explosion, the skiers and snowboarders that were too close, and the images of the smoke. Mud and stone reached high levels above the summit forming into the shape of a monstrous kraken. Poisonous gas clouds that immediately disable hikers. The 1996 eruption rippled through the ground, shooting miles into the air, raining down molten rocks all around. Ash clouds that you must lay down through and wait out.

Images you don't show Mom, before you ask to go.

He takes another look at the crater sleeping. Cold. Silent.

Is that steam? Is that smoke? Or is that fog? I hope that's fog.

Gentle streams of steam move slowly up from the blanket of fog that blocks the rest of the world from view.

My dad said, "Stick to the ski lifts, ascend the trail you researched and showed me, and come straight back down. Don't get lost in the fog. Don't get lost in the fog.

One last recording for mom, for friends.

"Tristan Hirt here at the summit of Mount Ruapehu, New Zealand, North Island, highest point."

Only his own face stares back at him. His Ray-Ban aviators with leather blinders made for his sixteenth birthday covered his eyes. No hat covered his short hair or ears. A Buff on his neck covered by a scarf showed all shades of blue just above his bright blue zipped Helly Hansen coat he stole from his dad after they had crossed the Atlantic to Cork in Ireland. Now he had crossed the Pacific. The other side of the world. Rocky points and fog filled the background of his face.

"I put a rock on the cairn here, right there."

Slowly the phone moves from his face to the pile of rocks to mark the summit. There are plenty of heavy-looking, hand-sized ones that make a pyramid. Some pebbles on top. One is his.

"I think it's around 9,177 feet. Started around 4 point 5 thousand feet. The ski resort, and, ah, ski place and walked up from there. There's no trail. It's all off trail. Right. February 27th, I believe. 2023."

He looks at himself. Smacks his gum. Checks his watch. Another gift from his father.

"The time right now is 1:35 pm. I summited at 1:26. I am now beginning my descent, and I will turn my phone off. So… Adios."

Bang. Rumble. Thunder.

Silence.

Is Ruapehu asleep? Was that all in my mind?

The smell of sulfur fills his lungs. He coughs.

The ski trail map flashes in his mind. The feel of urgency flashes through his nerves and disappears. He remains calm. All the lessons he has learned sailing in storms. He remains calm.

He descends slowly with careful steps. Coughs on the sulfur again.

Tūroa Trail Map. Higher than the top elevation of skiers. Above the Big Bowl, Snowbird, and Vertigo ski tracks. Follow the snow lift. Back down. Don't get lost in the fog. Don't get lost in the fog.

Mount Ruapehu

Harnessed with ski lifts, I am tied now.
My water melting in the heat of stay.
The clouds hiding me in their soup.
I'm embarrassed. Almost twice a year
I fight back erupting to let crawling,
sliding humans know, I will not be held.
Moving, growing, melting, thriving,
splitting, crying, shaking, screaming.
Sighing for my love, Taranaki, watching
him breathe in the west. I am shamefully
paired with Tongariro, my lover, but
always staring at Rua Taranaki, the pit
in me, he left behind. However, this
does not make me stagnate, calm,
useless. I'll. Stand. Freeze. Fall. Glacier.
Climb. Storm. Boulder. Avalanche. Break.
I welcome only purple mountain saxifrage,
birdeye pearlwort, and mirrorplant marble,
as I punish myself and let the humans ski.

Poor Knights

The dark side of the moonRises
and sheShows me a sliver of light

from under her skirt. Her lostLoves,
the poor knights islands, blinkWink,

and signal to her. NoResponse. She
rises further, further awayAttracted

to the stars and themToHer. Her shiny
skirt breaks out in a danceDown the aisle

of herReflection on the water. The coast
hides itself bathing in her darkSide. Wind

thrusts up the shoreWeathering igneous,
metamorphic, sedimentary, and herTease

continues. Like MarilynMonroe, she holds
down the fabricsOfCraters. She dares

the sunrise to dim her extravagantShow.
The poor knights lookOn getting further,

further away. Forgotten in herGlory.
BlinkWink, and signal. Nothing. The tide,

the ocean, all the creatures feelHerPull
and rise in herAppeal. The poor knights

whisper toHer about their arches, caves,
tunnels, fish thatInquire, sharks thatIngest,

dolphins thatTantalize. Nothing. Moon
is so far away now, sheReveals to tide

and coast her round, suppleLegs under
her shinySkirt. Tonight, she has been

distracted. Tonight, she could notResist
the attention. Tonight, sheDanced,

and she knew everyone wasWatching.

Bay of Plenty

I can't see the waves and wind
that pick up and toss me in the night,
but I can see into incalculable sums of stars
that pin the dark and shoot straight
towards me from unceasing space,
and I am the smallest creature soaring
over migrating rivers of great white sharks
under rivers of solar systems combined
into constellations that connect me
to everything, everyone, everywhere
with thoughts of warm slippers, cozy
sweaters, my husband's arms, and
in the middle of nowhere, you see
me reading this and keep me company,
as if the star that streaked the sky
was a rip in time, a zipper to connect
eyes of understanding, kindness, awe.

Marama. The Moon.

Born from darkness and ocean.

Carrying Rona — woman with gourd
and tree. Fill me with fierce fertility
and light. Open and close like a portal

for fighters, spirits, fires, stars, family.

The wind will spill from you shaking
my resolve, spilling my water, capturing
my essence. Marama. Momma. Moon.

Drop dreams of ancestors. I can catch.

About the Author

Magdalena Louise Hirt has a Master of Arts in English Literature from the University of Toledo and a Master of Letters from the University of Highlands and Islands for Scottish Highlands and Islands Literature.

Magdalena has multiple published articles in *Cruising World*, one in *Enchanted Living*, and another in *Literary Traveler*. Her first four poetry chapbooks, *Levels of the Ocean*, *Her Sea-filled Arms: Layers of Blue*, *Pacific Pieces*, and *Pacific Prescription: Leukemia Cyclone* are available for purchase. One more chapbook, *Her Bloody Project* is due to be released January of 2025. She has four self-published chapbooks, an article published via E-book from being a featured speaker at a conference in Oxford, and poems that have been published in *The Holland Sentinel*, *News from Hope College*, *The Mill* from the University of Toledo, and on display at the Toledo Museum of Art, which included first place and finalist awards. At Grand Valley State University, she received 1st place in fiction and 2nd place in poetry for the Oldenburg Writing Contest. She has been a featured speaker at a literary conference in Boston and two Poetry Speaks at the University of Toledo. She is currently finishing a script, a novel, and another poetry chapbook. With her teaching degree, she has taught Middle School Language Arts and Freshman Composition at the University of Toledo.

Currently, she homeschools her four children and writes from her sailboat, which is a Westerly 49, named *Selkie*. Their family of six sails to circumnavigate the globe. So far, they have cruised, wintered, and been through lockdown in the following locations: the Great Lakes of Michigan, the Caribbean, the Bahamas, Bermuda, Azores, Ireland, Scotland, Norway, the circle of the Baltic Sea, the Bay of Biscay, Canary Isles, Cape Verde, back to the Caribbean, the Dominican Republic, Guatemala, Panama, French Polynesia, the Kingdom of Tonga, and New Zealand. These locations completed an Atlantic circumnavigation and a Pacific crossing. Her family plans to finish a global circumnavigation by 2027 and continue to sail.

Magdalena enjoys cooking and dancing—most of the time together. With pen, spatula, and helm in hand, her sailing soul belongs on the sea where she chooses words, academics, ingredients, and destinations. Follow their story at www.sealongingselkie.net.

About the Press

Sea Crow Press

Sea Crow Press is an award-winning woman-run independent book publisher based on Cape Cod in Massachusetts committed to amplifying voices that might otherwise go unheard. We publish creative nonfiction, literary fiction, and poetry. Our books celebrate our connection to each other and to the natural world with a focus on positive change and great storytelling.